Entertaining Eric

Maureen Wells

Entertaining Eric

Letters from the Home Front 1941–44

Imperial War Museum

Published by the Imperial War Museum, Lambeth Road, London SE1 6HZ

Copyright © Maureen Wells 1988
Preface and Introduction © Trustees of the Imperial War Museum 1988

Dust jacket illustration by Marc

Designed by Herbert Spencer
Printed and bound in Great Britain by Butler & Tanner Ltd, Frome, Somerset BA11 1NF

Distributed by Leo Cooper in association with William Heinemann Ltd

Photographs
Maureen Wells Frontispiece, 163, 164, 165, 166, 168 (bottom), 169, 174
Pamela Burningham 170 (bottom), 171
Lady Rozelle Raynes 167 (bottom)
Countess Mountbatten of Burma 170 (top)
Margaret Boggis 167 (top)
Imperial War Museum 168 (top), 172, 173

Frontispiece: The author in 1943

British Library Cataloguing in Publication Data

Wells, Maureen
    Entertaining Eric: letters from the home front, 1941–1944.
    1. Great Britain, 1941–1944. Biographies
    I. Title
    941.084

ISBN 0–901627–41–0

Contents

Page 7   Foreword

9   Introduction

13   Author's Note

17   Part One   Billeting Officer 26 June 1941–20 October 1942

61   Part Two   Wren Courier 22 October 1942–26 September 1943

109   Part Three   Wren Stoker 27 September 1943–25 June 1944

161   Photographs

175   Courier Poem

Foreword

This is the ninth volume in the personal experience series produced by the Imperial War Museum and, like its predecessors, gives a vivid and lively account of wartime life. However, this book differs from the rest of the series in that it consists of personal letters written over a period of three and a half years and is not an account recollected in tranquillity. This gives it an immediacy and a freshness that is particularly attractive. Much of this is due to Maureen Wells's acute observation, sense of fun, and turn of phrase. She set out to entertain her fiancé and in doing so caught the flavour of the age and of her own experiences. She was clearly a young lady who could see the amusing and incongruous elements in any human situation and so wrote letters which, while in no way trivialising the subject of war itself, reveal that humour is an essential basis for dealing with hardship. Readers who lived through the war years will undoubtedly find much that is familiar in these pages, and younger generations will recognise a commonality of human experience: girls of today might well write letters of a similar sort to distant boyfriends, were it not for the ubiquitous telephone.

This book may also serve to remind people that the Museum continues to acquire letters, diaries, and other accounts relating to the various conflicts of the present century. Often people tell me that they have got some letters or diaries of their own, or of a relative, but of course (they say) these would be of no interest to the Museum. On the contrary, they nearly always are of interest and it is only by preserving the apparently inconsequential that we can build up an accurate account of the past.

Once again I thank my colleagues who have been responsible for seeing this book through the press. Dr Christopher Dowling, Keeper of the Department of Museum Services, has supervised the operation, with the tireless assistance of Mrs Janet Mihell. They form an excellent team and it is thanks to them that Maureen Wells no longer entertains only Eric.

Alan Borg, Director   February 1988
Imperial War Museum

Introduction

In 1985 a remarkable collection of long-forgotten letters was rediscovered in a box at the back of a garage in the Kooyong area of Melbourne. They had been written during the Second World War by Maureen Bolster, then in her early twenties, to her boyfriend Eric Wells. He was an Australian from Castlemaine, Victoria, who had come to England in 1937 to further his engineering career. She was the daughter of a surgeon commander in the Royal Navy and had trained as a fashion designer. They met at a wedding in London in March 1940 and fell in love. A few months later, on the eve of the Battle of Britain, Eric Wells was commissioned as a pilot officer in the technical branch of the Royal Air Force. At the end of the year he was posted to the Middle East.

Home leave was virtually unknown in the war and the couple were separated for three and a half years. During this period Maureen Bolster had three unusual jobs. As the billeting officer of a London engineering firm evacuated to a stately home near Guildford she faced the challenging task of persuading unwilling householders to take in industrial workers. After placing 1,200 men and women she volunteered for the Women's Royal Naval Service and joined a small group of Wren couriers, operating from Haslemere, who were responsible for the delivery of confidential dispatches and secret equipment to all parts of the United Kingdom. In the summer of 1943 she transferred to boats' crews, a special category of Wrens who manned harbour launches and other seagoing small craft. She successfully completed a boat drivers' course at the Mechanical Training Establishment, Portsmouth Dockyard, to become one of a select band of Wren stokers and in November 1943 was drafted to the crew of the captain's launch at HMS *Abatos*, Southampton. For the next seven months she served at invasion bases in the Portsmouth area during the preparations for and launching of Operation *Overlord*, the invasion of Europe, in which the WRNS played a notable part.

At least once and sometimes twice a week, Maureen Bolster wrote to Eric Wells to tell him about her experiences, to keep him informed of conditions on the home front and to express her hopes and fears for the future. But above all she wrote to amuse him and to make him laugh. *Entertaining Eric* consists of extracts from these delightful letters, which are not only moving, refreshingly uninhibited and often extremely funny but have an engaging freshness and vitality.

The story has a happy ending. Squadron Leader Eric Wells returned to the United Kingdom at the end of June 1944 on a posting to the Air Ministry and on 8 July he and Maureen were married at Compton parish church in Surrey. After the war they went to live in Australia where, as the author touchingly puts it, 'Maureen is still entertaining Eric.'

It is something of a miracle that this correspondence, which amounts to approximately 360 air letters and airgraphs, has been preserved. Eric Wells's duties as a staff officer entailed extensive travel in the eastern and western Mediterranean and newly arrived letters from Maureen went with him to such exotic places as Bahrain, Basra, Baghdad, Teheran, Mosul, Aleppo, Beirut, Algiers, Tunis, Fez and Casablanca. On his return to headquarters he filed them carefully in hard-backed loose leaf folders. Most of his luggage was stolen in transit between Tripoli and Cairo in August 1943 but somehow the letters got through.

Apart from the omission of irrelevant or trivial material and a few minor editorial changes the letters are reproduced as they were set down in Maureen Bolster's fluent and distinctive hand some forty-five years ago. The originals of four letters – those of 26 June 1941, June 1941, 5 June 1944 and 25 June 1944 – have disappeared and the text exists only in a transcript made by the author. For security reasons Maureen Bolster was not able to disclose the names of the bases she was writing from; these have been added for the convenience of the reader. The charming sketches with which she decorated her letters have been included where appropriate, as well as one or two drawings taken from a notebook she kept when she was a billeting officer.

In preparing *Entertaining Eric* for publication I have received enthusiastic cooperation and support from Maureen Wells, who kindly placed all the surviving letters at my disposal and, with Eric, answered numerous queries. I could not help noting in the course of our lengthy correspondence that my letters not infrequently took almost as long to reach her as Eric's did in the turmoil of the war years, a sad commentary on the modern postal service. I am also much indebted to four of Maureen's former cabinmates for the loan of photographs and for general advice: Lady Rozelle Raynes (née Pierrepont), who described her own experiences in the Wrens in her book *Maid Matelot*, published in 1971; Margaret Boggis; Pamela Burningham (née Desoutter); and Countess Mountbatten of Burma. Finally thanks are due to Ursula Stuart Mason, herself an ex-Wren and author of *The Wrens 1917–77*, who first drew my attention to *Entertaining Eric*, and to my colleague Janet Mihell, whose editorial assistance, as with previous volumes in the series, was invaluable.

Christopher Dowling
Keeper of the Department of Museum Services

For Eric, our children and grandchildren

Author's Note

The emotional effect of discovering the letters, unread for over forty years, was overwhelming. While I laughed and laughed, shed a few tears and winced occasionally at some of the youthful comments, I had a strong desire to share these findings. Thanks to the valued encouragement of ex-Wren friends I went ahead and in due course *Entertaining Eric* took form.

This is not a book about wartime heroics, nor is it memoirs. It is a record of how it was for one young English girl who wrote above all to entertain the man whom she loved. Often I felt strangely detached from her. Memories would intervene of things about which I had not written for fear of causing concern, such as air raids, the worst experiences as a courier and certain events leading to occasional confessions such as: 'It is only fair to tell you there is someone special in the Middle East!'

Thanks to the advice and kindness of ex-Wrens Pamela Burningham and Ursula Stuart Mason my book came to the notice of Dr Christopher Dowling of the Imperial War Museum.

This was the start of a remarkable and stimulating correspondence. I cannot speak too highly of the sensitive and detailed editing work done by Dr Dowling and his colleague, Jan Mihell. I am profoundly grateful to them.

Part One

PART ONE

Billeting Officer   26 June 1941 – 20 October 1942

26 June 1941   The Dykeries, Compton, Guildford, Surrey

Dearest Eric

I began a new job yesterday. It is really weird. The Labour Exchange sent me out to a nobleman's stately home which has been taken over by a big engineering firm evacuated from London. I went by bus to have an interview and it was quite an expedition. Big factory sheds are being built in the park under the trees (good camouflage) and the offices are in the house.

I had to see a fat and florid Major Blore, who is in charge of welfare. I told him I'd like a job on the bench, explaining about my mother being recently widowed and new to the neighbourhood.

He looked hard at me and said, 'No, that wouldn't be suitable. We need a nice young lady on the welfare.'

I panicked and told him I was only just twenty, my only experience was in *haute couture* fashion and design and ARP and I knew absolutely nothing about welfare. He wouldn't listen, and now here I am with the bewildering job of billeting officer. You see, staff and workers are still being evacuated from London and have to be housed in the neighbourhood. Lots of workers will be coming from all over England.

I have been provided with an autocycle, a red Rudge Whitworth. It makes a tremendous lot of noise. I have christened it Rudolph. My job is to go out and look for householders who will take in workers. It's awful that people have to take strangers into their homes. If I get hopelessly stuck the official billeting officer on the Rural District Council will help me, but I hope I don't have to ask. She seems quite nice but sees me as a rival. She wants billets mostly for children, and obviously people would rather take in workers who would be out all day and less nuisance.

So, my love, think of me in the butler's pantry with the pompous Major Blore, who does smell remarkably beery. I think I shall have some funny stories to tell.

June 1941   The Dykeries, Compton, Guildford, Surrey

Well, Major Blore really threw me in the deep end. He sent me to a big country house to see a well-known county lady. He hinted that he knew her socially, but I now have my doubts. It was awfully hot and I was petrified. I'd no idea what I was going to say and I wasn't sure of my facts either. A foreign woman came to the door and told me, 'Madame iss la, down de godden.' I looked in the direction of her pointing finger and saw Mrs S coming up the garden. She was elegant in pale blue and looked languid. She carried a flat basket of roses.

I swallowed hard and began. I was from Vokes and so sorry to bother her, but we were in urgent need of accommodation for war workers doing aircraft production. Unfortunately our firm's name is like that of a well-known dress firm and she thought I wanted to sell her some clothes. I took a deep breath and began again.

She was difficult, as you may imagine, but quite nice too, and agreed to take in a man, but he must be a *gentleman*, public school of course, and preferably university. She would see that he got a cup of tea in the morning, but could not provide dinner. He had better eat in the works canteen or a pub.

I returned to Major Blore very proud. I had landed my first billet!

Now an awful thing has happened. Major Blore told me this morning that a valuable tradesman was arriving and I must meet him at the station and take him to Mrs S. I asked him if he was the sort of man Mrs S had in mind and he said, 'Of course.'

One look at this Mr B and I knew the worst. Bowler hat on back of head, cheerful countenance, portly figure, loud sports jacket and dreadful tie. 'Pleased ter meetcher,' he said, beaming. I tried to prepare him as the works van drove up to his billet. He was so amiable, so pleased to be joining the firm, and he told me about his family.

As we came up the drive Mrs S appeared out of her imposing front door. I saw her glance at my companion and shudder. I introduced him. 'G'afternoon ma'am,' said Mr B, heartily extending a large hand. 'Pleased ter meetcher, I'm sure. Mighty kind of yer ter tike me in.'

'Oh,' said Mrs S. 'Oh.' Her hands rose in protest, then fell to her sides. She looked at me with despair. Silence. I suggested we go in. Reaching the drawing room, which clearly amazed poor Mr B, Mrs S asked him, 'Were you in the last war Mr...er...er...?'

'Lor yes, ma'am. Dispatch rider I was. 'Ere's a photo I 'ad took.' He handed a grubby snapshot to Mrs S, who could hardly bear to touch it. I left quickly. I don't know how this will work out and fear the worst.

I have a terrible lot to learn.

24 October 1941   The Dykeries, Compton, Guildford, Surrey

This is a bad week for me and my bike. Yesterday I had a skid and went over, the whole weight of the thing on top of me, and messed up my legs rather. Today I went out as usual and broke down miles from anywhere.

I hastily made my way to the nearest call box and phoned for someone to come from the works to help me. In the meantime, however, a policeman stopped and had a go at the machine, then another man joined us, then an AA man, so when our man from Vokes arrived there were five of us at it.

After about an hour they got it to go after a fashion. A party was decided upon and the nearest pub was visited *en masse*. Unfortunately

I had to make my way into Guildford so I said goodbye and off I went.

Just as I was getting into the town, pop, pop, bang, explosion, silence. I had to push the damn thing all the way to our Guildford works. It's in dock at the moment.

6 January 1942   The Dykeries, Compton, Guildford, Surrey

Lord, what a job this is! Would you like to be a billeting officer? Extreme tact and patience is necessity A and bright cheerfulness (even if you're feeling cold as ice) is necessity B. Lastly, but not least by any means, comes a sense of humour. That is vital. Also one must be physically fit. One mustn't mind getting soaked through, frost-bitten, blown about or over-tired.

Yesterday was quite a day in the life of a 'billeting lady'. Alarm goes off at 5.45. Turn over in bed and reaching out a hand in the dark push down the little trigger. Stretch, yawn, get up, dress, come down to cereal, coffee and toast by the kitchen fire. Put on the old leather coat, sling Gertie gas mask round me, grab my torch and out into the darkness. Wait about in the cold for the bus and wish on my star – if it's out. Clamber into the luxury coach hired by the firm and endure nasty pipes, coughing, noise and screeching factory girls.

WAITING FOR THE WORKS BUS.

Thirty minute journey, then through the big gates along the beautiful avenue to the 'bus stop'. Walk hurriedly to the staff clock and, grabbing card 10, clock in about 7.30. Upstairs to the cloakroom to tidy myself and hear office girls' conversation. 'Ow, Ethel, I didn't arf 'ave a good toime with Bert last night. 'E is a one! Did 'e kiss me? Oi'll say!' 'Isn't Miss X in the wages office a cat?' 'I saw Maisie in the pub with Jack last night. Dunno what Jack's wife would say.' 'Ain't that an awful jumper Doris wears?'

Go down to my office. Cope with any correspondence. I had a good one yesterday. 'Dear Miss, Would you please call and see me as soon as possible with reference to Mr Dearlove. Please excuse my writing in pencil but I am in bed with flu. Yours truly, Mrs Potter.'

Needless to say, for the sake of the people I associate with, I do not visit landladies who are in bed with flu.

The day before yesterday I billeted a man called Fingerhut. He was a foreigner of sorts taken on in the drawing office. When I went to tell him the address of his billet he asked me if there was a phone in the house. I said I didn't know. He turned round and said, 'Well, if there iss no phone it iss no good at all. You will haf to go and find me anoder billet.' I replied with all my dignity, 'I beg your pardon. Who do you imagine you're speaking to? I will *have* to do no such thing. If you want to change your billet I'm afraid you will have to look for your own.'

Yesterday I had a phone call from an irate landlord. Did I know I had landed them with a GERMAN, born in Berlin, only just released from internment on the Isle of Man and who had to report to the police every few days?

Dear oh dear. I had to spend half yesterday afternoon trying to pacify the poor wife. Apparently the man went there and said, 'My name is Fingerhut. I am a German,' and demanded this, that and the other – a fire in his room, special food etc. I think the poor little woman thought the invasion had begun! Anyway it turned out that the local police phoned the firm to say that he should never have been taken on.

You know, I often wonder how many men in the forces have any idea how their loving wives behave in their absence. Most of the women, even the very young girls here seem to be married but, my God, you'd never think so. Most of them seem to suffer from sex mania. There's one piece of work in the office who is married to a very decent lad in the navy – a jolly good type, too. He often gets a bit of leave as he's on shore duties and while he's there she's all over him – 'darling Hugh, dearest love' and all the rest of it, clinging round him like a vine. He thinks she's heaven on earth.

As soon as he's gone, however, she's out every night with one of the factory foremen and sits in the bus with him going to and from work holding hands. She makes no secret of it. She's been married four months and the foreman's a married man.

It makes you think.

9 January 1942   The Dykeries, Compton, Guildford, Surrey

My dearest

A word of advice. *Never* become a billeting officer. Half the employees of a firm gone bust are coming here next week. I am on the verge of hysteria, rushing round the country with the Rural District authorities trying to find billets which don't exist. The Labour Exchange is jumping up and down with agitation, the Rural District Council is at its wit's end. The management keep saying, 'We rely on you, Miss Bolster.'

Darling, it's chaos! The police are getting ready to issue compulsion forms. The awful part is that the men who are coming are well known as a lot of the biggest thugs going – racecourse touts mostly. I've grinned at so many landladies this week that my face is tired.

Besides the enormous crowd from that firm I've got others arriving from all directions.

Come and help me. Please!

17 February 1942   The Dykeries, Compton, Guildford, Surrey

Do you think you will ever see the Dykeries?[1] I hope so. I'll describe your room. It is small and square. The predominant colour is blue, the wallpaper is cream with blue sprigs on it, the curtains are blue, the bedspread is blue and cream. There's a cottage door to the room, a wooden one with a latch. The dressing table is a superb piece of furniture with a fine mirror. On the wall opposite hangs another large oblong mirror, which gives a lot of light to the room. There's a small table by the bed with a little electric reading lamp. There's

[1] Maureen Wells and her mother moved to the Dykeries in May 1941, five months after Eric Wells's departure for the Middle East.

a good chest of drawers and curtains hanging across two corners to provide wardrobe space. Above all, it is a friendly room. The outlook is lovely – fields and trees and the picturesque old dairy of Eastbury Farm.

I'd love to show you where I work. One day I will. We'll take the car and drive over. At the main gates, I'll salute the policeman on duty and, knowing me well, he will pass me through. We'll drive along the avenue through the wood, beneath magnificent trees, to the car park.

Arriving at the great mansion I will show you around – the ballroom, which is now a sea of drawing boards; the drawing room, which is now the sales office; the long panelled dining hall, now the planning office; the library, the head accountant's office; the lounge, which is now the firm secretary's abode; the morning room, now the general office – the junior accountant's next door.

Next the best bedrooms converted to Production Office, Maintenance, Buying, Inspection, the Big Boss; the billiard room converted to Wages and Costs. Then masses of dormitories for the clerks and typists, cloakrooms, mess rooms and the canteen quarters. The outside buildings, some new, some old, contain many more departments – the electricians, the stores, the jig and tool designers, Goods Inwards, Packing, Transport, Miss Bolster's office, the employment office, police office and so on. Of the places where production is carried on I'll say nothing. Out here in the country, surrounded by glorious park, one avoids the sordidness of industry. I could never work in an industrial town. Could you?

26 February 1942   The Dykeries, Compton, Guildford, Surrey

The amount of sneaking and tale-telling that goes on in this place is amazing. Here's a good example. The firm have just taken on a colossal mansion which belonged to Lord Boston. They intend to make it into a very large hostel for office and factory workers. (Sacrilege ... but still.)

Well, the day before yesterday a youth called Wilson was told to get the whole building measured up and the plans drawn by Saturday. He came and asked me if I could direct him to Monkshatch as it's a fair distance away and right out in the blue.

I told him that I was going over that day to make a thorough survey of the place and he'd better come along with me. On arriving, I checked up on everything I'd come to find out while Wilson got busy with his tape measure for all he was worth. He only had that day to measure up about fifty huge rooms. Out of ordinary humanity I said I'd help him for a couple of hours. Then I left him to it and returned to work. I thought no more about the incident.

Next morning I was sent for by the general manager. 'Miss Bolster, where were you yesterday?' I explained that I had gone over to Monkshatch.

'What were you doing at Monkshatch?'

'I went to check on certain things for the works manager, estimate how many beds it will take. I also helped Mr Wilson with some measuring as he was rushed for time.'

'I suppose, Miss Bolster, you realise what has been reported to me?'

'No, I have no idea.'

'That you and Mr Wilson deliberately contrived to go to that empty house and that you spent several hours there together. I leave it to your imagination what has been suggested.'

Do you know, Eric, I was so dumbfounded I couldn't speak. I just stared.

Fortunately the manager took my word for it! He knew I could be trusted all right but he had to ask me.

The ridiculous thing is that Wilson is weedy and anaemic and goes about wearing a balaclava helmet even in mild weather.

I was given a bit of a talking to and told that I must 'curb' my sense of humour! I wanted to say that if I hadn't had one I wouldn't have lasted in the job a week.

It all seems quite funny now but it naturally upset me at the time.

3 March 1942   The Dykeries, Compton, Guildford, Surrey

Yesterday was a glorious sunny springlike day here. Up at 6, I somehow couldn't get dressed quickly enough and had to run for the bus, hair flying, case in one hand, toast and marmalade in the other. Had a lot of people to see at my office over one thing and another. At about 11.30 I put on my various scarves, gloves etc and sallied forth on Rudolph. One of the men had cleaned him up for me and he was shining in his red paint with gold and black lettering.

Rudolph and I were both in good moods. He ran perfectly and

I sang at the top of my voice as I flew past trees and woods and fields and through villages to Guildford. Arriving there, I visited our other branch and, parking the bike, set off for the Ministry of Labour, where I did my business and chatted a bit with my friends. Then off down the High Street to the Rural District Council offices.

It was Mummy's birthday so bought her some bath salts, having also given her a library subscription for a year. Sent an air letter to you from the main post office, went to another place on business, then set off again on Rudolph. It really was lovely weather. Rode about seven miles looking for a certain empty house, then off to see a complaining landlady, going by a very pretty route. I must learn some new songs as Rudolph must be getting sick of my repertoire!

When I got back I at once applied to the Rural District Council for a requisitioning order to be brought against the house I'd found. Then I went to our weekly Ensa concert. It was a good one this week. A man who sang 'Over the Rainbow' rather well and played the saxophone, a couple of good tap dancers and a pianist. An amusing sketch was done.

I've been over to Ripley today – fourteen miles there, fourteen back. It's been another beautiful day and I sang lustily nearly all the way. Rudolph appeared to be a bit off colour – squeaked and groaned rather and at intervals shot forward in a most alarming manner. I haven't the faintest idea how he works. If he breaks down I'm helpless!

4 March 1942   The Dykeries, Compton, Guildford, Surrey

Mummy and I had a visitor yesterday. Catherine is the bossy WAAF officer daughter of one of Mummy's old school friends. She is a strong believer in free love for young girls and practises it. A year ago she fell most passionately in love with her commanding officer, a married man with a son of three, and they've been living together. She brought him down here once and I've never seen such a selfish, disagreeable-looking individual.

The next time she came she told me what a fool I was not to follow in her footsteps – wasting my youth etc etc. I brought up

all sorts of arguments but she was firmly convinced in her mind that I was an old-fashioned boop, a relic from the Victorian era. 'My dear, I assure you that 75 per cent of the Waafs will never see virginity again, and what's wrong? The men must go with somebody and the authorities prefer that they go with the Waafs, who are medically examined, rather than the women of the town.'

I gave up.

Last night she arrived quite late. To say that she looked haggard would be an understatement. She looked like death warmed up. Realising what was probably the cause of this, I made no reference to her Neville. Later she told me that he had dropped her just like that.

Quite honestly, I never expected anything else.

Although she didn't actually admit it, I can see that her views on free love for young girls (she's twenty-seven) are changing...

12 March 1942 The Dykeries, Compton, Guildford, Surrey

Dearest Brown Earwig

Is it awfully hot in the desert now? Are you sheltering in the shade to read this? Or in your palatial quarters? I wonder how you look. You are probably tanned, lightly clad, about the same as usual in girth and a little more mature in face and expression. Am I right?

I'm sitting in my office, christened 'The Abode of Love' by my friends the lorry drivers. I'm wearing a brown and white check tweed suit, a red jumper and American shoes. This is a bad drawing but then I have forgotten how to draw. It's quite chilly today. We've been having some sublime weather, then yesterday it had to go and pour with rain.

I've been out on Rudolph this morning and found it a bit cold for my liking. I'm now having my lunch hour, trying to decide whether it's worth making a sortie this afternoon, writing to you and waving to passers-by out of the window.

There's a tremendous feel of SPRING in the air! After one of the worst winters in living memory we have emerged into sunshine and comparative warmth (bar today) and the birds are singing loudly. I feel somewhat lighthearted (except when I read the papers) as I'm awfully susceptible to the spring. Also I've fitted in quite a lot of gaiety besides my fifty-six hours of work a week. Last night I went to a big hop in Godalming Borough Hall – a Home Guard

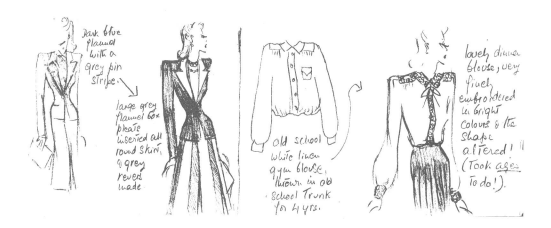

Dark blue flannel with a grey pin stripe.

large grey flannel box pleate inserted all round skirt, & grey revers made.

Old school white linen gym blouse, thrown in old school trunk for 4 yrs.

lovely dinner blouse, very finely embroidered in bright colours & the shape altered! (Took ages to do!).

affair, mixed and hearty and all that but good fun. There were sixteen of us and we were the only ones in evening dress! I feel a little bleary today, which partly explains my hesitation about going motorcycling this afternoon.

Typical remark when I arrive at work after a late night: 'Cor, miss, was you out with the soldiers last night?' To which one answers with as much dignity as one can muster, 'No, Mr Buggins, I was *not* out with the soldiers last night,' thus firmly closing the conversation.

Pat's twenty-first birthday present to me came last night, a lovely red rubber hotty bottle, a Boots 'snug'. Mine started leaking a few weeks ago and it's impossible to get them in the shops. It was terribly sweet of Pat as she went and ordered one through her firm, going to a lot of trouble over it. They're a terrific price now, the same as everything else. It's a queer sort of toothbrush you get for less than 2/-, hairbrushes cost about £1 at least and I had to pay 3/9 for a tiddly little nailbrush. Hair combs of any size at all cost 2/- (6d before the war) and large ones 2/6 or 3/-.

Hairgrips, tape, sewing materials and needles have to be scrounged. The one thing the shops do seem full of is toothpaste. Dress material is becoming poor, lingerie's an enormous price. One can buy lipstick fairly easily but hand cream and other creams are rare. Perfume is unobtainable apart from the 5 guinea per tiny bottle variety that no one can afford and is probably black market anyway. Still, one doesn't mind. They are such very minor details after all.

There is a beautiful spot not far from Compton, a valley where a river twists and turns, clear water reflecting trees and woods. There are high wooded hills, long open stretches, marshes a mass of kingcups, superb views from hilltops, little winding woodland paths leading up and down and round about, luxuriant grass and the ever flowing river. You would fall in love with it.

I'll take you there for a whole day when you come back. We'll have beer and cheese at an old farmhouse pub that I know of and we'll wander *ad lib* in this Garden of Eden. Then I'll show you Godalming one day – quaint, old and charming. And Puttenham Heath – miles and miles of pines, gorse and heather. And Puttenham village, each cottage prettier than the next, as in Compton.

We could take a bus from Compton Corner to Puttenham and walk up Lascombe Lane. That would bring us to the heath. Of course the weather would be wonderful. It'd have to be! You'd wear an open-necked shirt, your old slacks and jacket and I'd wear, if it was very hot, my fish and rope dress that you loved or, if it were just springlike, my gay plaid pleated skirt and dashing green jumper. Anyway I'd look nice!

There's no harm dreaming is there?

I caused quite a stir the other week when I was up in the buying department seeing one of the 'Bigger Buyers' about his landlady. We disagreed slightly on a matter concerning the payment. I was explaining my point in a reasonable manner, knowing what I was talking about, when he got impatient and broke in with a torrent of words – something like 'These bloody, buggerin' women comin' tellin' yer wot ter do about yer own billet. To hell . . .' etc etc.

I merely looked at him, turned round and walked out of the office quietly, to the delight of all the clerks and typists. I reported the matter to Mr Willis, who agreed that I was not here to be sworn at. The said Big Buyer has avoided me since.

We've sold the car to the Rawlplug Company and got £260 for it. Out of that we've got to pay a commission to the dealer who wangled it for us. I got on to him through my great friend George Mitchell, the transport manager.

I love old George. He tells everyone that I've got the best figure in the firm and that I get better-looking every day. He's always wanting to know when I'll go and 'ave a noice quiet weekend with 'im. In front of a whole lot of people the other day he called out as I was passing, 'There goes Esther Bolster, the only girl in the firm who's pure. I'd have a night with 'er myself if I could!'

Loud laughter ensues. I endeavour without any success to look dignified.

I am practically down to my last clothing coupon so, as I wanted a petticoat, I went into a furnishing shop in Guildford today and asked for some thin silky material for a large cushion cover. I got some lovely blue satiny stuff, blackout proof, which will do for a glamorous underskirt.

I don't know what was the matter with me yesterday. I said the wrong thing to a landlady. She was telling me how she'd had a young soldier's wife there, who'd left because her husband had been posted and she could not sleep alone. 'Goodness,' I said, 'whatever was she doing before she married?'

The landlady giggled weakly, then pursed her lips and looked grim so I quickly changed the conversation to strictly business.

ME IN MY RED GOWN!

31 March 1942   The Dykeries, Compton, Guildford, Surrey

I've got a sweet boyfriend. He lives in Puttenham and always sits with me in the bus. His name is Mr Turvil and he giggles 'he, he, he'. His sense of humour is delicious and he loves to come out with snappy and naughty bits of scandal about the locals.

Relations of his are maids in some of the big houses around. The others in the bus tease me as he always pushes to get on, then makes a beeline for me. He flirts too. Last night I said that I'd heard that one of the village girls had made a pretty bride on Saturday.

'Oh,' said old Turvil, 'I don't think so. You'd make a better, that you would, he, he, he.'

3 April 1942   The Dykeries, Compton, Guildford, Surrey

Oh dearest

I'm so cross! What do you think? We've been working 7.30 am to 6.30 pm every day with an hour for lunch and till 12 on Saturdays. Now we've got to do 7.30 to 7.15, only thirty minutes off for lunch, and do till 12.30 on Saturdays. It's the absolute limit. Imagine twelve hours or so a day actually at work.

Did I ever tell you how I went to a certain village to do a door to door canvass in the summer and how I went to a house with a large garden at the back? I walked round there to find the front door (it was that sort of house) and in the middle of the lawn, sunbathing, was a naked woman. All she'd got on was sunglasses. Embarrassed to tears I made a getaway but I had time to see she wasn't a bit exciting – about forty and all saggy!

Then there was the first time I had to cope with an immorality case. I'd been here about three weeks and a letter from a landlady came to our department to say that she had a pair of brothers billeted on her along with their first cousin, Molly. Immorality had occurred and she wanted us to do something about it. Old Blore went and put the job on me, the old cuss. He said that it was for a woman to deal with it. I pleaded that I was barely twenty and a half and had no experience in such matters – but to no avail.

Freda ran me down in a little green van. I was terrified. I hadn't the faintest idea of what I was going to say. The woman turned out to be quite nice and young and at last I got the whole story out of her.

Oh, dearest!

I'm *so* cross!!

What do you think?

We've been working 7.30 a.m. To 6.30 p.m every day with 1 hr for lunch, & Till 12 on Saturdays. Now we've got to

The Dykeries,
Compton,
Guildford
Surrey.

3-4-42.

She'd been landed with these two brothers, aged eighteen and sixteen, both gipsy and rough to a degree. She had put them both in a double room, to share a bed. The cousin, aged seventeen, had come and implored her to take her in, saying she was just like their sister. Mrs C being a kindly soul (and needing the £sd) put her in a small single room two doors away from the brothers.

Sister, my foot! Every night when the house was quiet Mrs C and her husband heard creeping in the passage. The younger brother and the girl were swopping bedrooms so that the latter could get in the double bed with the elder brother. One night, though, they were caught red-handed.

But the best of it was — Mrs C was herself living in sin as she and her 'husband' weren't married at all! I told her to give them notice and that they would not be allotted other billets. She did so.

Later the girl's mother paid me a visit. Filthy dirty and looking even more like a gipsy than her daughter, she told me in not too polite language that 'er gal was absolutely pure — like a sister she was to young Dave. Never 'ad a dirty thought in 'er life.

You'd need to see the daughter.

Then there was the dear old soul who was asked by an ATS girl if she'd take her in. She put her in the best bedroom with lace curtains and whatnot. Then the girl asked if she could bring her husband. Dear old soul didn't like to refuse. 'Husband' came. They never paid rent, or never enough anyway. Later the landlady found they weren't married after all. He had a wife and three children in Edinburgh. She gave them notice. They left without paying and the room was so spoilt she had to send the furniture and bedding to be cleaned.

The dear old soul now has two nice respectable elderly men with whom she chats of an evening by the fire. She mends their socks and everyone's happy.

I get offered cups of tea all over the place. One woman the other day, upset because I said I never drank tea, offered me coffee. Longing for some, I remembered the drastic milk rationing and refused. Cocoa? No thanks. Then it was soup, then sherry. Tempted, I went away as it wouldn't do for a billeting officer to partake of alcohol on her rounds, even though she *was* rather cold.

I'm becoming expert at baby worshipping. 'Oh, isn't he beautiful, so bonny. Lot of hair he's got for his age. What? It's a girl? I'm so sorry.'

Then there are the people with dogs which bark. I went to a row of bungalows the other day. Halfway down there was one where the door was opened by a woman holding by the collar a colossal dog of indeterminate breed. It didn't stop barking for a second and she made no attempt to restrain it. I had to scream that I was from so and so limited, which was in urgent need of accommodation for workers. By the time I'd finished the rest of the row were well prepared for me. The whole lot of them were 'out' when I rang. Not another door was opened to me.

Then there are the amiable sort of people who are stone deaf and don't inform you till you've brought out all your patter and persuasion. Having been smiling complacently they put their hand behind one ear and say, 'Eh? I can't hear you, dear. I'm deaf.' Taking a deep breath and feeling dreadfully weak, you begin all over again.

Naturally one hears the most exciting, lurid, amusing, dirty, sad stories on one's rounds. One sees how other people live, how they keep their houses and all the rest of it.

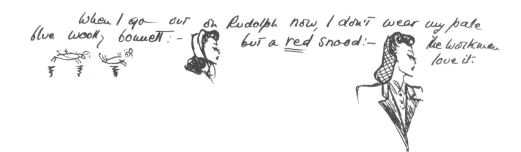

When I go out on Rudolph now, I don't wear my pale blue woolly bonnett :— but a red snood :— the workmen love it.

28 April 1942   The Dykeries, Compton, Guildford, Surrey

Darling

I'm so *terribly* proud of you – you've no idea! A squadron leader already and you've only been in the RAF a year and a half! I can't get over it. Mummy and I wondered if you'd get promotion on taking over after the group captain's exit. I wish I could tell you now, this moment, how glad I am. Anyway, it's terrific, magnificent and stupendous! Your family will be so proud of you. Squadron leader does sound *grand* doesn't it? Don't become a wing commander yet, dearest, as I might be frightened of you!

Oh, I've just realised – I've put flight lieutenant in the address. Aren't I a cuckoo?

1 May 1942   The Dykeries, Compton, Guildford, Surrey

We are always having minor excitements on our works bus. If it's not getting stuck halfway up the Hog's Back it's catching fire or something like that. Last night as we approached the end of our lane I stood up to get my case down from the rack. A lorry in front stopped suddenly. The bus pulled up with a terrific jerk and I was thrown right into the engine.

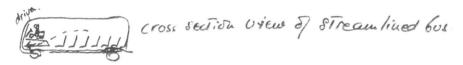

Cross section view of streamlined bus

I was flung from beside the third seat back to the very front and I was so tightly wedged between the engine and the protrusion caused by the mudguard that two men had to heave me out. I nearly collapsed with faintness. I recovered after a few minutes, walked home and forgot about it – except for a few minor bruises. Today, however, I had queer twinges round the bottom of my right ribs and the worst is feared.

The doctor is seeing me tomorrow morning to tell me if the rib is fractured or not. It doesn't really hurt an awful lot. I went to work as usual but didn't go out on Rudolph.

2 May 1942   The Dykeries, Compton, Guildford, Surrey

Dr Cliff Hodges's partner came to see me this morning. I liked him – he was reasonably young and human. The verdict is several bruised ribs and most probably one cracked, if not more. I am swathed in enormous pieces of plaster from my middle front to my middle back. It does feel queer – like a mummy or something. I'd draw you a sketch of how funny I look but it wouldn't be modest or proper. I shall probably be able to go back to work in seven or eight days' time but mustn't ride Rudolph for a long while. It'll be nice having a rest. I shall get through all my mending and make myself a dress.

8 May 1942   The Dykeries, Compton, Guildford, Surrey

These are genuine extracts from letters sent to the Public Assistance Committee:

1. I cannot get sick pay. I have no children. Can you tell me why?
2. Mrs B had no clothes for a year and has been regularly visited by the clergy.
3. Unless I get my husband's money I shall be forced to lead an immortal life.
4. Please send money at once as I need it badly. I have fallen into error with my landlord.
5. I have no children. My husband is a bus driver and works day and night.
6. I want my money as quickly as possible. I have been in bed with the doctor for a week and if things do not improve I shall have to get a new doctor.
7. I am very annoyed to find that you've branded my child as illiterate. It's a dirty lie as I married his father a week before he was born.
8. Please find out if my husband is dead for the man I am living with won't eat or sleep or do anything till he knows.
9. In answer to your letter, I have given birth to a little boy weighing ten pounds and hope this is satisfactory.
10. Dental enquiry. The teeth in the top are all right but the teeth in my bottom hurt terribly.

34   Not bad, are they?

27 May 1942   The Dykeries, Compton, Guildford, Surrey

Last Thursday Mummy and I sallied forth by the 9.06 bus to Guildford, boarded a train and came down to London. I wore my red jacket. Also a little black hat on the back of my head with a little red feather. This, however, I soon changed as in Swan and Edgar I saw the most dashing white fez with a blue tassel and couldn't resist it. We had a very enjoyable and fruitful shop crawl, had lunch, then went to the Piccadilly theatre to see Noël Coward's *Blithe Spirit*. Everyone was looking at my fez as I walked in. I'm sure you'd fall for it as it's very sweet.

As for the play, dearest, it was terrific. I wish we could go and see it together. It's a farce – about a man whose wife dies so he marries again (Fay Compton). They decide to have a dinner party and ask one or two people including an eccentric old woman called Madame Arcati, who professes to be a spiritualist. They persuade her, for fun, to hold a seance and by accident, after performing weird rituals, she conjures back her host's first wife. Kay Hamond plays the spirit, in grey wispy chiffon and painted entirely grey – just like a ghost, most effective. The difficulties the man gets into, having a spirit and a real wife, are extremely funny and cleverly worked out.

The dialogue was absolutely Noël Coward.

1 June 1942   The Dykeries, Compton, Guildford, Surrey

There's a terrific purge going on at the firm. Seventy employees were transferred by the Ministry of Labour last week including several High Ups on the office staff. It's all very unsettling and one wonders when one's turn is coming. I should hate to find myself in Leeds or Birmingham.

The tension in the firm is considerable.

4 June 1942   The Dykeries, Compton, Guildford, Surrey

Dearest Eric

Summer has come! It's very hot. The sun pours down. Underfoot it's dusty and the men are working stripped to the waist. I am wearing my 'jungle' frock that you liked so much and very little else.

Everyone is lethargic and inclined to laziness – me too! Still, it's far worse for you. At least we don't have sandflies though there are lots of long wiggly grass snakes that terrify me stiff and lots of bugs that bite. Please inform the sandflies from me that they are to leave you alone and not to pester you as I simply won't have you bitten!

Everyone's thrilled about the thousand-plane raids on the Ruhr.[1]

8 June 1942   The Dykeries, Compton, Guildford, Surrey

A great pal of mine is Walter O'Brien, maintenance labourer, who comes and cleans my window. He sits on the sill for hours, telling me about his affair with Nurse Foster from a local hospital.

He's really hideous – like a little bird – and his skin is all marked from gas in the last war. However, he's a dear is Walter and he calls me his 'sweetie miss'.

His *affaire d'amour* has been most complicated. She'd been wanting an engagement for ages but he couldn't make up his mind if she was after his money or not! However, last week he was wavering. She was thirty-four and he was no chicken himself so perhaps . . .

'Look here, Walter,' I said on Friday. 'You take Nurse Foster out tomorrow. It's June, lovely weather, and what could be more romantic than Newlands Corner.' (Famous local beauty spot.) 'Take her up there and pop the question when the moon comes out.'

'Oh,' he said, 'shall I?'

'Yes,' I replied, 'and come and tell me the result on Monday.'

This morning a radiant Walter appeared at my window. Ow, 'e was hengaged 'e was! Lovely ring an' all, cost four pounds and a few tanners. Diamonds 'twas – yeah! Reely! And she gave 'im a lovely kiss – boy, was 'e 'appy. And she was comin' fire watchin'

---

[1] On the nights of 30 May and 1 June a thousand bombers raided Cologne and Essen respectively in the greatest aerial attacks mounted up to that time.

on Wednesday night with 'im. Three months hengagement, that's wot it's ter be, yeah.

Dear oh dear. I hope Miss Foster is worthy of Walter.

12 June 1942   The Dykeries, Compton, Guildford, Surrey

Dearest Eric

Heard quite a good yarn this week. Portsmouth had been bombed. The King (in the uniform of an admiral of the fleet) and the Queen were doing a tour of inspection. They came to a very badly blitzed street where there was just one house left standing. It seemed to be occupied so the Queen suggested to the mayor and corporation that she and the King should call on these people alone.

They knocked at the door. A little girl appeared. 'Is your Mummy in, my dear?' asked the Queen. 'No she ain't,' was the reply, 'but she left a message to say that when the girl with the sailor came they could have the front room for an hour for a tanner.'

16 June 1942   The Dykeries, Compton, Guildford, Surrey

Life here goes on much the same as ever. I paid twelve visits yesterday and got nine billets. Ordinary day's travail. Mrs Bettingdon is staying with us for a fortnight and I find her rather depressing. She thinks silk stockings are degenerate! She asked me if I ever wore those 'shocking chiffon nightdresses' (very transparent ones). I replied, 'No, but I would if I were married.'

In her opinion I am far too 'flibberty jib'.

17 June 1942   The Dykeries, Compton, Guildford, Surrey

Dearest Eric

I'm exhausted.

I've just come in from an inter-factory netball match. I played centre attack against a great coarse creature called 'Etty. Besides being exhausted, I am also crippled. I shall borrow a pair of footer boots off one of the workmen and play in them next time. Anyway, we won 6–4.

Really it is awfully rough here. The pitch is not at all as it should

37

Me having bath.

Me playing netball.

Me playing Tennis.

be and this is the first time I've played for five years. I used to be good then. I played for Wadhurst against Roedean (the girls' Eton), the Tunbridge Wells Ladies Club and lots of schools. Then one played the game as one should play – swiftly, lightly and with skill. Here one barges, shoves, pushes, kicks and gets the ball as best one can.

But the exercise is good for one.

This morning I called on a very agreeable woman in a hideous semi-detached villa. After showing me with pride her few and badly furnished rooms, we sat on the sofa and proceeded to discuss the wherefore and why of taking in war workers. One thing led to another and I stayed far longer chatting than a billeting officer ought to.

She was an Australian, hailing from Melbourne. Her husband is still out there and she was amazingly interesting. She cannot wait to get back and can't think why she ever came to England, even for a holiday. A most comfortable, homely and cheery woman – one who would make even the most shabby household seem a palace.

One day I shall make an excuse to call on her again.

22 June 1942   The Dykeries, Compton, Guildford, Surrey

Dearest Eric

There's been a major tragedy on the home front – we've lost Sandy. He died on Saturday morning after a short illness (poisoning) and though the best vet in the district attended him nothing could be done.

I was horribly upset about it as I really loved that little dog. So did Mummy. He was the grandest chap.

Joy is all alone now and fretting terribly. Sandy had lots of friends in the village, from Mrs Jupp at the little shop where he lodged when Joy was in season, to the occupants of the manor, who used to enjoy taking him for walks.

He'd become quite an institution.

7 July 1942   The Dykeries, Compton, Guildford, Surrey

I did have a lovely time yesterday. In bright sunshine I set off from the works on Rudolph, clad in a print frock and light tweed coat. Before I'd got to Guildford down came the rain. An absolute deluge! I was soaked to the skin in a second.

Cars had to stop and I alighted and ran under a tree. I could feel little rivers runing down my chest. My shoes were full of water and my clothes were clinging to me.

Then it calmed down a bit so I decided the only thing to do was to pop home and change and get a mack. Shivering, I got on Rudolph again and swung on to the bypass. I was halfway home when another deluge occurred.

I couldn't go on. There was nothing in sight to shelter under – not a tree, not a bush – nothing but the open highway. It began to hail. I just stood there holding on to Rudolph's handlebars, my head bent, my collar turned up. My hair streamed. Harder and harder came the rain.

Suddenly it stopped and turned to a reasonably mild patter. I went on home and you should have seen Mummy's face when I arrived. I undressed in the kitchen so as not to make a mess upstairs. Not half an inch of me was dry.

The worst of it was that when I got back to the works in different clothes no one would believe what had happened as they hadn't had a drop of rain there.

Such fun, the life of a billeting officer . . .

All my love to you,

Love,

Laureen.

✗ ✗✗✗ ✗✗ ✗ ✗ ✗ ✗ ✗ ✗ ✗ ✗ ✗✗✗ ✗ ✗✗ ✗ ✗✗ ✗ ✗✗ ✗✗ ✗ ✗ ✗ ✗ ✗ ✗ ✗ ✗

9 July 1942   The Dykeries, Compton, Guildford, Surrey

Dearest Eric

I went out billeting yesterday and visited a council cottage. The front door looked like one of those that are never used so I went round the back. I was just going to knock when the window above opened and the contents of the dustpan descended on yours truly. I was enveloped in a cloud of black filth. Then I found it was the wrong house – not the one I wanted at all.

I have an idea the householder thought I was the rent collector.

17 July 1942   The Dykeries, Compton, Guildford, Surrey

Well, my dearest, I've been and gone and done it – I've volunteered for the navy. I've airgraphed you to explain how and why I'm making this move, willy-nilly, by instinct. I just knew I had to do it – it was some force stronger than me – and I don't think I shall regret it. It had been coming for a day or two, then on Wednesday it became uncontrollable. I found myself telling the National Service officer that I wanted to go and was surprised at my own voice.

I rode back to the works and went to see Mr Willis. I told him that I would like to go in the navy and would he very much mind if I left? He said he minded a lot and I'd be a great loss to the firm but as he had daughters of his own he understood and would not stand in my way.

He really couldn't have been nicer. He said that if I failed to get into the department I wanted I could always come back. He gave me permission to go up to London the next day (yesterday) so I got on one of the lorries and went to the Wren HQ. I was interviewed by a charming young woman who said they'd accept my application as it was very hard to find experienced motorcyclists but of course I must go through the usual formalities.

Back I came yesterday afternoon and contacted the Ministry of Labour again. They told me that unless I produced relations in the navy I'd never get in and they couldn't help me. Today I went there with a nice letter from the firm withdrawing their application for my exemption and a list as follows:

Father
    Surgeon Captain F Bolster CMG MD RN (deceased)
Surviving Relatives
    Captain Charles Bolster DSO RN
    Lieutenant J Bolster RN
    Lieutenant D Bolster RNVR and
    Paymaster Commander R Bolster RN
References to
    Admiral Sir Lionel Halsey CB KCMG RN
    Vice-Admiral Molteno CB RN and
    Mr T Willis c/o Vokes

Next I should be summoned for my medical. That does not frighten me. Then I go for interview.

The first move is training at a south coast port. There are very few dispatch riders indeed and they are a complete speciality – 'the darlings of the navy'. One is taught by a dirt-track rider who sits on the pillion at first. The test is hard and thorough.

You are attached with a couple of others to a port and you run about all over the place. You take dispatches to battleships and hand them to the captain. You go to airfields and hand them to the officer commanding. All traffic gives way to you. You don't have to work very long hours, 9-5 as a rule. The equipment provided is superb: breeches and shiny leather leggings and a tailored jacket nipped in at the waist. Unfortunately a crash helmet as well. Then for cold weather a great big lined windproofed mackintosh.

You get two ordinary Wren outfits with special markings to show your superiority over the rank and file. When you've been qualified three months you get wings (don't know why).

July 1942   The Dykeries, Compton, Guildford, Surrey

Another applicant came up for my job last week. I had a phone call from Clarke, the interior welfare officer, asking me to go up to his office. I found him interviewing a specimen of the female gender. She was about thirty-five, small, slight and filthy dirty. Her pale blue dress was marked all down the front and was remarkably greasy. Her hair was untidy and streaky. Moreover there was an unpleasant pungent smell pervading the office. The clerk behind the desk in the corner was wrinkling her nose like a rabbit.

41

I asked to see the woman's application form. Education – elementary. Profession – nurse till marriage. Address – little cottage in the village. I knew she was hopeless from my first glance at her. However, at Clarke's request I took her over to my office to explain the work to her.

The atmosphere in 'The Abode of Love' quickly became unbearable. I opened the window wide, feeling horribly sick.

She was quite pleasant to talk to. I've no doubt she would work hard and be conscientious, but she would never have the flair, the personality or patience and tact for the job. She would be totally incapable of coping with the irascible Lord B or the aristocratic Lady P. If confronted by insults from a cottager she'd no doubt retaliate in the same language.

When Mr Clarke asked me what I thought of her I said that I did not think she would make a suitable billeting officer and that she was not sufficiently clean in her person.

'Oh?' said Clarke. 'I didn't notice anything.'

The girl in the corner gurgled, then came out with the quite witty remark, 'Oh no, an ideal BO!'

24 July 1942   The Dykeries, Compton, Guildford, Surrey

Have you heard this silly story? During a geography lesson the mistress asked the class, 'Where does one find mangoes?' A little boy put his hand up. 'Please, miss, where woman goes!' I expect you know it.

I had three breakdowns on the bike this week and was furious with the mechanics. I told them they wouldn't be able to mend a perambulator.

25 July 1942   The Dykeries, Compton, Guildford, Surrey

Holiday begins at twelve. Nobody's working and people are wandering round from office to office to chat with friends.

I started well this morning. I'd no sooner taken off my coat and sat down when there was a knock at the door. Enter one of my landladies complete with umbrella and an enormous hat, which drowned even her portly figure. 'Miss Bolster, I've 'ad no pay from Mr Mewett this week. 'E's gone off and not a penny 'ave I seen and

42

I won't be treated like that. I'm a decent British citizen and I'm entitled to my money same as everyone else is and I'm not goin' to move off these premises till I gets it!'

I rang the bell and sent a lad to get Mr Mewett up from the factory.

God, what a fight ensued!

'Let me tell you . . .'

'Yer don't deserve a sou, yer ol' bitch!'

'I'll report you to the Ministry of Labour.'

'Pigsty of an 'ome you've got.'

'I've worked meself to the bone lookin' after you.'

I acted as referee and the final result was Mrs X marching off, twenty-four shillings more in her bag than when she came in, followed by Mr Mewett looking sulky and grumbling nineteen to the dozen – something about 'these bloody women'.

Last night I came home and saw a familiar-looking buff-coloured envelope lying on the table. An airgraph from Eric, hurray! No? Lord, what's this? Oh heavens, it's nothing of the sort. It's my first income tax demand!

30 July 1942   The Dykeries, Compton, Guildford, Surrey

Before I tell you anything I must ask you to investigate the top left hand corner of this page. Don't I smell nice? I do, don't I? Perfume has been off the market for over a year but when I was in Marshall and Snelgrove's today buying soap I asked if there was any perfume at all, knowing it was a silly question. The girl looked at me and smiled. 'Well, madam, it's not made any more you know but I have just one bottle left of the last quota we'll ever have in.' Don't ask me how much it was, dearest, (I didn't tell Mummy) but you see it was exactly the same as the precious French perfume I used to wear for your benefit. It's unbelievable but although this is a different make completely it's absolutely indistinguishable. Sniff and see!

On Tuesday I took the train to London and went to the Wren HQ at Westminster to ask if I could be called up as soon as possible. When they told me it might take months I came out scheming like mad to find a way of pulling strings.

Then I wandered into Westminster Abbey. Sunlight streamed down in hazy beams. The fine roof seemed so high and distant, its ageless grandeur and tranquil atmosphere more pronounced than I had ever known it. One or two windows had been knocked out by bombs, otherwise it was intact.

Afterwards I made my way to Piccadilly and visited the 1942 Royal Academy. I consider it the best since the war began. The Russell Flint oil temperas, the Dodd portraits and several obscure works gave me a lot of pleasure. I wish I'd had more time there.

At 12.30 I arrived at the Normandie Hotel for lunch with Monsieur Blanchard. He really is a supreme example of the elderly *distingué* Frenchman, with perfect manners, a quiet wit and good conversation. I adore him, he's so small and cherubic, and he does love to talk to someone in his own tongue. I'm the only person he ever talks to at the firm. It was almost pathetic the pleasure it gave him to take me out and he certainly did it well. Cocktails, then a swagger lunch with Sauterne. After which he took me to see the most wonderful film, *Mrs Miniver* – I've told you in an airgraph how much I enjoyed it.

He's such a lonely little old man as his wife's been in hospital for two years and will never come home. He's been all over the world, knows Australia inside out and stayed some weeks at Castlemaine, which he loved. Like other people he assured me that the hospitality there is something unknown in England. Australia, and Victoria in particular, sound so wonderful that it seems strange people should want to leave it!

Next morning I decided to go over to Farnham to visit Daddy's old friend, Admiral Molteno[1] (with string-pulling in mind). When I reached Farnham I found that I had a three mile walk to my destination. It was a nice morning so I didn't mind. At last I got there and found it was the most beautiful big house on a hill top, surrounded by pine woods. A really idyllic spot.

As for the admiral and his wife, they were so delightful I can't describe them. Their pleasure at seeing 'Bolster's daughter' was unbounded. They said it was so long since they'd seen anyone 'young and pretty' that it was an occasion. The old boy walked me round the garden, showing me this and that, and Mrs Molteno was so sweet, with a sort of spontaneous kindness that you don't often meet. I interested them enormously by expounding on the state of affairs in industry at the moment and by talking a lot about the control of wages, supply difficulties and 'bottlenecks'.

---

[1] Vice-Admiral Vincent Barkly Molteno, 1872–1952. He commanded the cruiser *Warrior*, in which Frank Bolster was ship's surgeon, at the Battle of Jutland. The *Warrior* was badly damaged in the engagement and had to be abandoned.

Do you remember those two big prints of the Battle of Jutland in the dining room at Monkton?[1] Admiral Molteno has the two originals and our prints were done specially for Daddy as a present from him.

It was a most pleasant day.

4 August 1942   The Dykeries, Compton, Guildford, Surrey

Did I ever tell you about Millie and Effie? Well, Mrs Tubbs is a very nice little woman who lives in a village close by. Her cottage is scrupulously clean and very old-fashioned – texts on the walls, antimacassars and all the rest of it.

She agreed to take in two girls for me, so I sent her two inspectresses. One was enormous – known at the works as 'Two Ton Annie'. Her real name was Millie. The other, Effie, was a thin little thing, like a mouse. They seemed to settle down very well.

Then, one day I had a note from Mrs Tubbs asking me to go and see her.

'Cor,' she said, 'they don' 'arf fight! Fatty keeps accusin' Effie of

[1] The Bolster family lived at Monkton, Biggleswade, Bedfordshire, from 1924 until Frank Bolster's sudden death from pneumonia in February 1941.

takin' up too much room in the bed. Did you ever 'ear anythink ser daft?'

Moreover Millie was always being superior. She was a lidy, she was! 'Course, at my 'ome we 'ave a proper lav. My pa *never* goes without a collar.'

This annoyed Mrs Tubbs very much. 'And I says to 'er, miss, I says, "*You* ain't no lidy, as reel lidies never talks about being lidies. They expects yer to tike it fer granted!"'

'Quite right, Mrs Tubbs,' I replied.

The next thing was that Millie and Effie came to blows in the bedroom and the latter was knocked completely out. Mrs Tubbs gave Millie the sack and kept the other. Effie, however, soon left and went to someone else who was a notorious gossip and spread some dirty stories about Mrs Tubbs round the village.

10 August 1942   The Dykeries, Compton, Guildford, Surrey

Dearest Eric

Have I had a morning! I was asked this week if I'd attend a meeting at the borough municipal offices and agreed, not thinking much about it. I got there and found it was a big bugs' round table conference in the council chamber! The head welfare officer for the Ministry of Labour for South East England and his deputy, the town clerk and head billeting officer for the borough, the head billeting officer for the rural area, the head of the local Ministry of Labour and his deputy, the employment manager of Dennis Brothers, the welfare officer for Drummond Brothers and little me, representing Vokes.

I wasn't expecting anything like this, I can tell you. I came through it all right. It lasted two and a half hours.

17 August 1942   The Dykeries, Compton, Guildford, Surrey

Dearest Eric

Am I thankful that I volunteered for the Wrens when I did! I knew at the time I was meant to do it and that there was some influence urging me. Last week all the single girls of around my age were told they had to go – even those with indefinite exemption such as I've got. They're taking on no more unmarried workers and are going to rely on part-time labour and married women only. All these girls who are called up have to join the ATS! I simply can't get over my luck.

They've told me that I'd have had to go with the others if I hadn't volunteered already.

Most industries are now doing the same thing – married women for the factories, single women for the services.

you & me
jitterbugging
at Henlow.

18 August 1942   The Dykeries, Compton, Guildford, Surrey

Dearest Eric

At last we have a little summer! Yesterday was the first day of sunshine we have had for weeks and weeks. One had got to the stage of craving for the sun – for warmth and light – and as grey, muggy days followed each other one became more and more lethargic, sleepy and exasperated.

Last night we heard the sensational news that Churchill has gone to Moscow.[1] You know, one of my first thoughts on hearing this was that he might have stopped at Habbaniyah. It would have been such fun for you to see him – perhaps even talk to him. I'm longing to hear from you if you have.

I wish I'd known he was going as I'd have applied to have gone too! Do you think they would have let me?

'Now, madam, and what is your business out East?'

'Oh, very official and important.'

'What is the exact nature of this business?'

'MEWH.'

'And the meaning, please?'

'Making Eric Wells Happy!'

---

[1] Churchill flew to Moscow from Cairo via Teheran on 12 August to give Stalin the unwelcome message that there would be no Allied landing in France in 1942. He later described his mission as 'like carrying a lump of ice to the North Pole'.

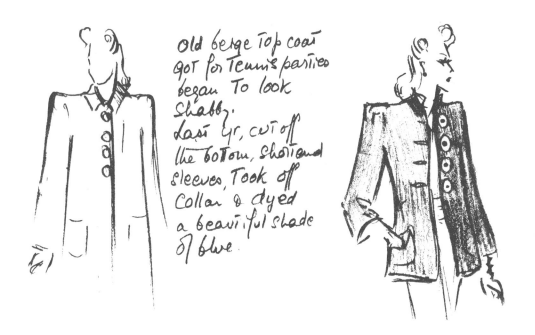

Old beige Top coat got for Tennis parties began To look Shabby. Last Yr, cut off the bottom, shortened sleeves, Took off Collar & dyed a beautiful shade of blue.

19 August 1942   The Dykeries, Compton, Guildford, Surrey

News *was* interesting this morning. Big raid in progress on France. We're all wondering if it's the real thing or not. If it is, life will be exciting enough for a while.

One awaits the one o'clock news with much impatience.

I hope that, if I become a dispatch rider, I shall get over to France when we invade. There will be a tremendous lot to be done in the way of propaganda.

Later: Alack, our landing in Dieppe is not invasion but a large commando raid. Our men are still over there – thrilling![1]

26 August 1942   The Dykeries, Compton, Guildford, Surrey

Dearest

I had a visitor in my room last night – the most enormous and horrible spider I've ever seen. It had a great fat body and long thick

---

[1] The Dieppe raid was one of the most costly single operations of the war. The raiding force, which consisted mainly of Canadian troops, was unable to capture the town and, after nine hours of fierce fighting, withdrew as planned. Well over half of the 5,000 Canadians were killed or taken prisoner.

legs. I was simply paralysed. And when it moved – that nearly finished me. I've never seen a spider like it. Ugh! I don't really mind little ones but big ones scare me stiff.

Had a letter from the WRNS on Monday returning my birth certificate and saying that they will arrange for me to go for a medical and an interview as soon as possible. Today Mr Willis, as one of my referees, had a form from them asking *terrible* questions. Was I absolutely to be trusted with vital and secret work? Was I entirely honest and trustworthy? Did he consider I was a suitable person to undertake the responsibilities of a dispatch rider for the Wrens? Would he recommend me to his most intimate friends? Oh, yes, and did he consider I was a person of the Highest Integrity?

I must say it's a smashing reference he has given me.

3 September 1942   The Dykeries, Compton, Guildford, Surrey

Dearest Eric

The third anniversary of the outbreak of the war. Really, it can't go on much longer can it? I am in bed with a horrible bilious attack and feeling very weak.

It's a day of national prayer and Mummy keeps rushing off to church. They were going to have a big open-air service in the park at Vokes. I rather wish I could have gone. They asked me if I'd sing in the small choir they got up. I said thank you very much but the only time my voice sounded nice was when the bath water was running.

9 September 1942   The Dykeries, Compton, Guildford, Surrey

Dearest Eric

A happy New Year to you, my love.

I did so hope the war might end this year and you come home. But it's too much to expect now. Perhaps next year . . .

Somehow the whole of 1942 up to this has been a sort of stagnation period. Nothing particularly spectacular has happened in the war, has it, apart from the great Russian battles? As far as I can see, except for having more materials and losing a bit of land out in the Far East things are little different than they were at the beginning of the year. We've made fools of ourselves in Libya, mounted one or two commando attacks on the enemy coast, carried out some magnificent bombing raids and been hopelessly whacked in Malaya, Burma, Hong Kong and in the Pacific. We've also got into difficulties in India.

One can only wonder what 1943 has in store for us.

11 September 1942   The Dykeries, Compton, Guildford, Surrey

I've begun to train a new billeting officer. I can't make her out quite. She's not exactly well-bred but very passable – about forty, single, small, slight and rather sweet-mannered. She's capable of doing the job, finding billets and pacifying householders but I'm afraid it'll be some time before she'll stand up to the workers when they become aggressive. She's a bit on the timid and fluttery side. She might faint if an immorality complaint came in.

I've had a great time taking her round. 'This is Miss Barnes, my successor.' Everyone keeps saying, 'Oh, Miss Bolster, you *will* come back and see us, won't you?' or 'You *must* come and show us your dispatch rider's uniform,' or 'Do let us know how you get on.'

I don't expect they'll ever see or hear of me again.

11 September 1942   The Dykeries, Compton, Guildford, Surrey

Yesterday I rode a pukka motorbike for the first time. One of the lorry drivers, an Australian actually, offered to teach me before I go in the Wrens so I joyfully accepted. I was absolutely terrified. It was a nasty great black thing and more complicated and heavy than Rudolph.

It was going pillion that scared me – I didn't mind when I was in control. Geordie sat on the back and held on to me like a clamp, ready to grab the controls if I did anything wrong.

He told me I was an excellent pupil. Soldiers passing by thought it all a great joke. Actually my hands weren't big or strong enough to work the clutch very happily.

16 September 1942 The Dykeries, Compton, Guildford, Surrey

I had a terrific day yesterday. I arose at 7.15, dressed in a pretty cotton frock and long coat and set off for Guildford by the 8.20 bus. Had a little time to fill in before I was due for my medical at 9.15. Met one or two friends *en route* for work and hobnobbed with them. Very punctually I wandered into the big building by Trinity Church. I sat on a row of chairs with some other girls all trying for the Wrens. They were a queer lot – a VAD from Aldershot, a miss who'd been brought up in Singapore, a girl from a leather factory, a professional tailoress, one or two who looked like servants and a few others.

After a short wait I had to go into another room and be interviewed by a welfare officer. Had I ever had TB? Mental disorders? Nerve trouble? Rheumatic fever? Had my parents ever had any of these? Were there any of these in the family? What illnesses had my brother had? What did my father die of? Had any of us ever been in an asylum? Was I receiving any compensation for injuries? And a whole lot of other similar enquiries.

When we'd all been interviewed we were marshalled upstairs to a great hall. We were each given a small cubicle and told to undress entirely keeping only our topcoats on. Then we all sat on a row of chairs at the back of the hall. They started with me (B for Bolster) and I was sent in to see the woman doctor. She was about fifty something and very horsey. She went all over my back and front with a stethoscope and I deep-breathed interminably. I had to do heaven knows how many exercises – toe touching, leg kicking, arm waving, stretching and bending. Then she made me lie flat on the bed while she pummelled my tummy.

'Does that hurt?' she asked.

'No,' said I bravely.

'Well it should!' she snapped.

She got all excited about the scar on my knee (souvenir of a fall from a cliff in Ireland when I was six) and made me do all sorts of things to prove that the joint wasn't affected.

By the time she'd finished with me I was exhausted.

Then I was pulled into another cubicle to be weighed and measured. I was 9 stone 11 lb. Have gone up a bit.

I was just going back to my chair when I was sent into another cubicle for something unexpected and unmentionable. At least I didn't have to drink nearly a jug of water as one girl did!

Next I went before a man doctor. The first question he shot at me was, 'How many fits have you had?' Didn't ask me if I'd *ever* had any! Afterwards I realised that the answer was, 'Only this one, on seeing you!' He had a good go at me – nose, throat, ears, teeth, eyes. I'm very proud as I was the only girl who could read the bottom line in the eye test. And he asked me a whole lot more questions. He wanted to know all my past medical history and goodness knows what else!

Then I was ushered into the presence of the President of the Medical Board, Surgeon Vice-Admiral Sir Basil Hall.[1] I sat down in the chair in front of his desk. He was a small elderly man with a rather benevolent air. I liked him. He said nothing at first, poring over my papers. Then, 'How did you come to be born at the Royal Naval Hospital, Bighi?' I told him that my father was stationed out there. He looked at me for a moment. 'Good God! You're not Frank Bolster's girl, are you?'

Wasn't it marvellous? Daddy had served under him for quite a while and they were firm friends. We chatted for a bit, then he said, 'Perhaps we'd better get down to business,' and the palaver and questions began again.

I then had to go and dress and await my interview with the Wren officer. While I was waiting Sir Basil came along and beckoned to me. He was awfully sweet and wanted to know about everything. When I said, 'Please, *have* I passed my medical?' he winked an eye and whispered, 'Grade 1 plus!'

The other girls were apt to be a bit sniffy, presuming that I was using influence – maybe they were right but I couldn't help it!

I had a bit of a wait for the interview. We sat in a room with a Wren who gave us the lowdown on the service. Poor girl, we *fired* questions at her. The Wrens are allowed to wear black silk stockings now ... goody goody.

At last I was ushered into the August Presence. She was as ugly as can be but so nice. She really couldn't have been kinder. She began by saying, 'I see you want to be a dispatch rider.'

'Yes,' I said.

'My dear, isn't that rather a waste with your domestic economy and welfare experience?'

[1] Surgeon Vice-Admiral Sir Robert William Basil Hall, 1876–1951. Medical Director-General of the Navy, 1934–1937. Chairman, National Service Medical Board, Guildford, 1939–1944.

I explained it was that I was trying to get away from! She wanted to put me in quarters (looking after all the other Wrens) but agreed that I was really too young as they're mostly girls of twenty-five and over who do that. She said it would be kinder to let me go with the younger ones. She said I seemed to have done a tremendous lot of things for my age.

I asked if there had been any accidents or deaths among the WRNS dispatch riders. She said none had been killed but one or two had had accidents. Each proved to be their own fault – speeding. Well, I'm not a speed hog at all. It's only the night riding and going out in very heavy frost and snow that will worry me.

She asked me what books I read and all sorts of questions. I was with her about twenty minutes. Then I escaped and fled down the High Street as fast as my legs would carry me.

I'm hoping to be called up in a couple of weeks and may have to go at a moment's notice.

20 September 1942   The Dykeries, Compton, Guildford, Surrey

No, dearest, I don't think we should get officially engaged till you come home. There is just the risk that we may find each other changed for the worse. Having made it all public we might not be strong-minded enough to stop it and awful consequences might occur.

Actually I've no fear at all that such a thing would happen. I'm sure that it'll be just as it always was and better, as both of us have matured and learnt so much more and done so much more – if it wasn't the 'real thing' we wouldn't be writing to each other now.

And don't you think all the charm of getting engaged would be lost if we were apart? I think it's something to be intimately shared. Imagine the fun of reading together the following announcement:

> **Squadron Leader Wells** RAFVR **and Miss Bolster**
> The engagement is announced between Eric James, eldest son of Mr and Mrs Wells, 'Derwent', Castlemaine, Victoria, Australia, and Esther Maureen, only daughter of the late Surgeon Captain F Bolster CMG MD RN Retd and Mrs Bolster of the Dykeries, Compton, Surrey.

we Tickling you!

Amazing the way my mind works, isn't it?

24 September 1942   The Dykeries, Compton, Guildford, Surrey

I have done my last day's work for Vokes! It's the wonderfullest feeling, really it is. I'm on leave till my call up papers come, then I go back for one day, put my official release through and bid farewell to my acquaintances. There are one or two I shall be sorry to say goodbye to: Mr Turvil, who cleans the lavatories, Mr Willis, of course, as he's been the grandest boss anyone could ever have, George Mitchell, the Cockney transport manager, some of the lorry drivers and a few in the factories.

To have a week or two at home! The bliss of it! To have time to do things I like doing. But it's a sobering thought that this is the last stretch of home life I'll have for the duration.

25 September 1942   The Dykeries, Compton, Guildford, Surrey

There's a lovely miniature of Daddy in naval uniform on the desk in front of me. He was amazingly handsome in a very distinguished sort of way. It's funny to think that it's his daughter who's following in his footsteps, not his son. I wonder what he'd think of me going into his old (and much beloved) service. I'm sure he would be very proud of me though a little perturbed. I wonder if he knows what I'm doing – I feel he does somehow. I'm afraid that my career won't be as brilliant as his was. I'll probably get the sack for being too high-spirited or having too much sense of humour or for forgetting to salute or something.

Have you heard the story of the American and the WVS? An American soldier was walking along Piccadilly when he saw a large placard saying 'WVS Recruiting Depot'. Puzzled, he asked a policeman, 'Say, pal, just what do those letters mean?'

'Women's Voluntary Service,' was the reply.

'Thanks, pal,' said the American and made a beeline for the door. A few minutes later he came out and returned to the policeman.

'See here, buddy,' he said. 'I'd rather pay.'

28 September 1942   The Dykeries, Compton, Guildford, Surrey

There, do you hear that noise? Bump, bump, crash, bump. Do you know what that is? It's chestnuts being blown off the big tree by the house. They crash down the roof and bounce on the ground. It's such a row, it keeps waking Mummy up at night.

It's all very autumnal now – cold, dreary and misty. The trees are fast turning yellow and squirrels run about on the lawn picking up hazelnuts. I love them, they look so sweet, but Mummy always shoos them away. It's pouring with rain as usual, and rivers are running down the path. The nights are cold and as fuel is scarce one doesn't have fires yet, so we sit swathed in rugs by an empty grate.

Yesterday Mummy and I took baskets and went collecting faggots and sticks in the wood like a couple of gipsies.

6 October 1942   The Dykeries, Compton, Guildford, Surrey

I have certainly had a busy day. I was roped in to sell flags for St Thomas's Hospital, as today was All Hospitals Day. A friend called Ruth Appleton[1] and I represented Thomas's on Waterloo station under the jurisdiction of the Marchioness of Hamilton.

I went up early and began at 9.30. I had the run of the station and accosted everyone in sight. An American negro with nice manners and an RAF officer asked me out to dinner on the spot. Both invitations were politely and firmly refused!

I approached an elderly couple, the wife loaded with furs and *diamanté*, the husband kindly and prosperous looking. He bought a flag and put 2/6 in the box. Then, looking at my elephant necklace (which I was wearing on my red jacket) he said, 'My word, I do admire that. Do you mind telling me where it came from?' I replied that it was from Ceylon.

'Come along,' said the wife, 'you mustn't stand talking to that girl all day.' He shrugged his shoulders, looked again at the elephants and was led off.

Fat women with pet dogs and preoccupied businessmen snubbed one, soldiers and sailors called me 'darling' and 'beautiful' and gave sixpences, rich-looking women looked down their noses, poor women gave freely.

ATS and Waafs were stingy, porters and policemen generous.

It was all experience.

---

[1] Daughter of Arthur Beeny Appleton, 1889–1950. Professor of Anatomy, St Thomas's Hospital, University of London. Professor of Anatomy, Royal Academy of Arts.

10 October 1942   The Dykeries, Compton, Guildford, Surrey

Dearest

Exactly a fortnight and not a line from you! Whatever has happened? Are you ill? Have you been sent elsewhere? Are you on your way home? (Vain and idle hope!) This silence is most perturbing and I don't like it at all.

We had a grand Red Cross dance at the village hall on Wednesday. Tickets were 1/6 and I took a party of thirty. Not bad for wartime, is it? Everyone thoroughly enjoyed themselves and drinks were flowing in the Harrow Inn next door.

It was quite the local social event of the year. Rich people in the neighbourhood gave donations or sent modest refreshments. The rest of the community at the dance, besides my big party which included Angel Knox and medical students, were village girls and soldiers. Mummy climbed up amid the band to present raffle prizes and spot dance awards.

I do wish you'd been there. It was all such fun.

15 October 1942   The Dykeries, Compton, Guildford, Surrey

On Tuesday I plucked up my courage and went back to Vokes. I duly paid my farewells and came away with a present of just over £5 from the firm. Now that it's all over and I've really left I realise how much I'd grown to loathe it. I hadn't let myself think about it while I was there – I just went on day after day – but now my feeling of relief at leaving is overwhelming.

I shall never go back.

18 October 1942   The Dykeries, Compton, Guildford, Surrey

Dearest Eric

Nearer and nearer draws the time. I have been indulging in an orgy of washing, ironing and sewing on name tapes. Everything must be clearly marked as thieving is rampant in the WRNS, the same as everywhere else. Have just learnt that I'll be given three blankets only – one below and two above – and that the pillows are filled with straw! I shall pass out from cold and discomfort.

I am experiencing the same emotions as I did before I embarked, aged twelve, on my first term at Wadhurst College. I keep thinking a lot about school these days. How I hated all the pettiness and catty feuds and fights of the female community and the thousand and one rules and regulations.

I wish you were here. I need moral support. Do write to me a lot, please write a lot. Think of me doing PT and saying 'Yes, ma'am,' 'No, ma'am,' and doing motorcycle tests and living in most uncomfortable conditions.

Oh Lord.

20 October 1942   The Dykeries, Compton, Guildford, Surrey

My dearest

This is the last letter I shall write to you as a civilian, at least for the duration. Tomorrow I embark on the Great Adventure. I have to report at the WRNS training depot in Southsea between 2 and 4 pm. Do you remember your last night as a civilian – Sir Henry Wood, Vosne Romanée and the Ouse beneath the stars? I wish mine could be as perfect: here I am spending it quietly with Mummy.

Now about letters. You'd better go on sending them to the Dykeries and Mummy can forward them. Then, as regards mine to you, my output in airgraphs will not diminish but I may not have the same facilities for posting them that I've had up to now so don't be surprised if they come more in batches.

As for long air mail letters, I fear I shan't be able to afford one every week, dearest. I only get 13/- to begin with. However, I will see what I can do. In December I'll be able to start sending you air mail letter cards.

Keep on writing to me, won't you? Your letters will mean even more while I'm away from home.

Part Two

PART TWO

Wren Courier   22 October 1942 – 26 September 1943

22 October 1942	WRNS Training Depot, Bowlands, Southsea, Hampshire

Strike a light, sink me. This is like Wormwood Scrubs. Am now Probationer Wren Bolster, WRNS Training Depot, Bowlands, Southsea. I came down yesterday and have had a nasty shock. Two days ago the Admiralty ordered that no more dispatch riders were to be taken on because of all the accidents, so here I am, desperately anxious to know what's going to happen to me. My one year's clean licence may push me through. There's nothing else I want to do and I'd simply set my heart on being a dispatch rider.

Bowlands is just like school – strict discipline – and we're all enveloped in navy blue overalls buttoned up to the neck. There are six in my room, sorry, cabin, and we have sort of bunk iron beds on top of each other. Below me is a girl who snores like a pig. One of the others is hopeless – blathers and simpers and does singing and breathing exercises all the time.

I'm quite enjoying it, actually. We have masses of lectures and squad drill. I was picked out this morning by the instructor as the smartest and had to be marker.

23 October 1942	WRNS Training Depot, Bowlands, Southsea, Hampshire

Yesterday we marched in squad to the naval barracks to have our bosoms radiographed for TB. Much booing from sailors but we'd been instructed to take no notice. One hardly has time to think. I'm dying to begin dispatch rider training but it'll be a few days before I know what's going to happen to me.

Last night a girl I've palled up with a bit, June Burgoyne – an RAF officer's wife – and a girl who was at the Paris Academy with me went out and had sausages and chips in a funny little restaurant with another Wren, who turned out to be a great friend of everyone around Compton.

It's always being drummed into us that we are vastly superior to the ATS and WAAF as they're only auxiliary services and we're really part of the Royal Navy. Today we had a lecture and were told that sailors and naval officers do not like glamour!

The new Wren hats are smashing. The modern Wren is the smartest of all uniformed women.

23 October 1942
WRNS Training Depot, Bowlands, Southsea, Hampshire

Dearest

My first instinct when I have a second to myself is to write to you. It gives me a sense of proportion. I'm duty Wren today so am 'confined to barracks'. My other airgraphs were written in crowded rooms full of giggling girls and were probably not coherent.

I'm agreeably surprised by everything. Conditions are excellent, girls on the whole not bad. We've already had masses of lectures all about the navy and ranks and categories and traditions and what to do and when. The officers are nice but, my God, what efficient women! It simply bowls you over. But they're more genial than the petty officers. *Their* fierceness is indescribable. It's worse than any school marm's.

I was whispering a funny story in the cabin after lights out last night and in came one of the beauties.

'Girls, what *do* you think you're doing? Monstrous behaviour. Bolster, was that you?'

'Yes, petty officer.'

'You will kindly refrain from being an infant and realise that you are hoping to be enrolled in His Majesty's Navy. Any more nonsense and you'll go to the first officer!'

Everything's terribly naval – the kitchen's the galley and the dormitories are cabins. I'm in 'Dolphin'. The bunks aren't bad but the pillows are awful and I didn't sleep a wink my first night – girl snoring beneath me, wind screaming over the sea, funny mattress, straw-filled lumpy pillow and cats carousing outside.

My pal Christine Cooper, who was at Vokes and is now a dispatch rider at Portsmouth, dropped in last night and, gee, was I pleased to see her. In the whole depot I'm the only applicant to be a dispatch rider. All the girls goggle at one. 'Ow, aren't yew brave!' 'Can you *reely* ride a motor bike?'

For the first two weeks we have to be in our cabins by 9 and lights out is at 10. Up at 7.30 but when you're duty Wren you're up at 7. Oh dearest, you should have seen me today polishing the cabin floor and scrubbing the mess room tables. It's so character forming!

The technical name for a probationer Wren like me is a Sprog.

	WRNS Training Depot, Bowlands,
28 October 1942	Southsea, Hampshire

Dearest

Do please come and rescue me! I'm wondering if I've bitten off more than I can chew. It's only by the grace of God I'm here writing to you. On Monday I was called for by the CO. 'Bolster, you are being allowed the privilege of training as a dispatch rider if you pass a test. You will be the last allowed to do this in the command.' I was bucked no end!

Yesterday, feeling scared stiff, I tootled round to an enormous garage to meet my instructor and have a test. Mr Jock Sheppell is an ex-dirt-track rider and very decent. He gave me a crash helmet and a dispatch rider's coat, and took me pillion on to the front.

The first thing I had to do was something I'd never done – turn round on the spot. Sticking my legs out in all directions I managed somehow. Up and down I had to go, backwards and forwards in a high gale.

That night Mr Sheppell had to report to C-in-C Dockyard on what I was like. He's passed me. This morning I had to go to the barracks for a vision test. Eyes are A1.

This afternoon I was given helmet, breeches, coat and gloves. 'That's your bike, miss. You get on and follow me.' It was a Triumph 350 (I am only used to the 250) with a completely new gearbox. I wobbled along through the town behind Mr Sheppell. I had to stop for traffic and the darn thing conked out. A policeman waved me on, people stared, I got hot and bothered and a little boy said, 'Cor, look at 'er. She's one of them Wren dispatch riders.'

Eventually I got going, then the fun began. I followed Mr Sheppell for miles. He did all sorts of antics, slowing down, darting forward, shooting round corners, and he made me speed so. Honestly, I've never had such an afternoon in my life. He made me do 50 mph on my first tour.

Actually being a dispatch rider has its compensations. I'm the only one in the whole depot and am rather a speciality. I don't have to do chores and I get off all lectures and squad drill.

5 November 1942   HMS *Mercury I*, Haslemere, Surrey

Have left Southsea and the training depot and am now at Haslemere. I explained how, after a bit of difficulty I got permission to have a dispatch rider test. I passed it and then began two weeks' special training. Last Thursday the first officer (my CO) called for me and told me that she had a very important and responsible job to offer me, that it was a great honour to be chosen and that she advised me strongly to take it. It was to be a 'confidential courier', to go anywhere in the British Isles at any time, travelling by plane, car and train and taking things too vital for posting or sending by dispatch riders.

I didn't know what to do. I wanted to be a dispatch rider and work with Chris and her friends yet this sounded a much better job. I went away and thought it over carefully from every aspect, then went back to the CO and told her I'd have it.

Last Sunday I went home for the day. Monday was lovely – I went on an excursion across the ferry to Gosport in the morning. In the afternoon I played my very first game of hockey and amazed the field by rushing away like the wind and shooting a goal. After tea I was officially enrolled for the duration as a Wren. No turning back now!

On Tuesday we trooped to the RN barracks and got our uniforms. I really don't look bad in mine. The hat is very sweet and my topcoat is slick. That evening we all had a farewell binge at a restaurant, none of us wanting to leave – it had all been so clean and nice and friendly.

And now, here I am with one other girl at Haslemere. We are out in the blue. It's impossible to go anywhere at night as there is no means of getting back – we are miles from a shop, bus or cinema.

I am in a cabin with fourteen others, all couriers. Except for this other girl who's twenty-five none are under thirty. Six are over forty! They're tough and strong and ugly. They've taken no notice of me at all except to ask me what on earth I think I'm doing here at my age. Their conversation is dreadful. They all hate each other and are fighting among themselves like a lot of cats. There are other

Wrens here besides couriers but not one whom I could talk to.

The cabin is revoltingly untidy – greasy hairnets hanging on bedposts, drawers bulging, clothes on the floor. (The depot was spotless.) The whole atmosphere of the place is terrible – cold, grim and unfriendly.

19 November 1942   HMS *Mercury I*, Haslemere, Surrey

My job is far from glamorous with winter on the doorstep. At the moment I'm waiting all dressed, packed and ready to go off to … but I musn't tell you that! No one knows except me and my boss.

25 November 1942   HMS *Mercury I*, Haslemere, Surrey

Have just come back from twenty-four hours at home, spent sleeping! I had a really wonderful round tour, including a very very special experience. I've been aboard a big destroyer and was entertained with a great deal of gusto by all the officers to cocktails and lunch in the wardroom. I was the only woman on board. That's something which happens once in a blue moon and to very few. I was shown all round the ship and thoroughly enjoyed the whole thing.

When I went out to the destroyer I had to be lifted aboard and that exonerated me from saluting the quarterdeck! Everywhere I went on this trip I got free meals and was well entertained. But it's seldom one's so lucky.

27 November 1942   HMS *Mercury I*, Haslemere, Surrey

Further adventures of a hobo. I was called out late one night for an urgent job. My instructions were to position myself in a conspicuous place on a London station meeting a given train in the early hours of the morning and to contact a naval officer carrying a green suitcase.

Half the navy seemed to be on that station and all were carrying green suitcases! I have never seen so many suitcases of that colour in my life. I kept on asking and accosting and the last person off the train was the right one!

65

Then hurroosh – scramble and rush for a taxi. I had to catch a certain train going to Wales. Only just managed it. Long tedious journey, boring people in the carriage. The business transacted, off to a Wrennery for a meal, my first in twenty-four hours. I was faint from hunger. Spent a really delightful evening among the most friendly lot of girls imaginable. Up very early, into the train again. I was luckier than when going as I found myself with a most entertaining and talkative carriageful.

Such is my life, dearest. Here one day and gone the next.

7 December 1942   Royal Hotel, Thurso, Caithness

Do you know, on Euston station I glimpsed an RAF officer and my heart turned over inside me and went thump, thump, THUMP. I thought it was you. Eagerly I went forward, not daring to hope, as if in a dream. Then it wasn't you and I sort of subsided again but the likeness was remarkable.

I don't know what he thought of me gaping and staring at him. He got in the train and I carefully avoided that carriage, feeling embarrassed. I felt quite weak when I sat down.

11 December 1942   The Dykeries, Compton, Guildford, Surrey

Dearest

Home! My first long weekend leave since I went into navy blue. Have you had my other letter card telling of my journey to the north of Scotland? After Inverness I came on to Thurso. Next morning there was a wonderful sunrise, the sky all green and gold.

During the day an RN car called for me and took me down to the boat. The sea couldn't have been bluer, there wasn't a cloud in the sky and faintly in the distance the Orkney Isles gleamed pink through the mist. I felt very elated, conscious of the glorious adventure of it.

Did you know that the crossing to the Orkneys is the worst in the world? That people can travel anywhere on the globe and not turn a hair yet succumb to this one?

The weather was too good to go below so I stayed on deck, took off my little sailor hat and let the wind play havoc with my hair. After a bit I was horrified to find people being sick all around, first one then another. I went below. I was the only woman aboard and had access to the officers' lounge. Dear me, what a sight – hardened naval men looking too green for words. Every few moments someone hurried up on deck. There certainly was a swell but it didn't affect me.

After an hour and a quarter a steward came up and asked me if I was all right. I told him I was and he very kindly suggested that if I felt like it I could lie on his bunk. Feeling that if I saw anyone else being ill I'd be ill in sympathy I took advantage of his offer.

I went first to an island, a green wild place, where the only women they ever see are the handful doing my job. A hard, desperate life with few comforts. I was regaled with coffee and sandwiches and, an hour and a half later, set sail for Orkney. Across the water the bugles were sounding for sunset. The isles were all pearly and misty and the sun went down in a blaze of red and gold. It was like a dream.

Do you remember that awful time when that German submarine sneaked into Scapa Flow and sank the *Royal Oak*?[1] I saw just where it happened.

I was met at the landing stage by an RN car and taken to the

---

[1] On 14 October 1939 U-47 penetrated the defences at Scapa Flow and sank the battleship *Royal Oak* as she lay at anchor. More than 800 officers and men were lost.

Wren quarters at a Fleet Air Arm station. They're a specially picked lot of girls up there and they were simply sweet to me – hospitable wasn't the word. They've lovely quarters and I was treated like a queen. Some of them asked me if I'd go to the cinema with them, so I went. We sat in a row, six Wrens in an audience of enthusiastic barracking sailors. Lor, it was funny. You couldn't hear a word of the film for all the noise. It was Ann Sheridan in *King's Row*. Then we came back and drank hot cocoa in the fo'c'sle. Afterwards I went to my bunk and fell asleep with the wind howling and howling.

Next morning I looked round a bit. It's a queer wild bleak spot but fascinating withal. There's not a tree up there, nor flowers, nor bushes, just rolling hills and a clean outline against the sky. There's no civilisation at all. The gales are so strong that great lorries are blown like leaves and large sheds are lifted into space.

The Wrens have a great time, though, as the social life is terrific. I was invited to a coffee party in the motor transport hut and thoroughly enjoyed it.

On leaving that I embarked on the biggest adventure of all, my first plane flight. Thrilling all over and scarcely able to contain myself I clambered in and sat on a form against the side of the plane, having to twist sideways and look over my shoulder to see out. I couldn't wait for the take-off and my excitement caused a little amusement among fellow passengers.

There was a superb sky and flying over the Orkneys was something I'll never forget – then over the sea, then over north Scotland. I was in heaven. Somehow it seemed the most natural thing in the world to be airborne.

But this bliss was not to last. Over the Highlands we ran into black clouds and a gale. The plane was just like a leaf in the wind – and those air pockets. Oh, dearest, my poor tummy! I hated them so!

I began to feel rather 'disturbed' and noticed everyone else turning vaguely green. It was impossible to speak for noise. All at once I realised that I was going to be sick (as two others had been) and a kind sailor helped me to the back of the plane. Leaning on a crate for support, I suddenly became aware that we were going down and, exerting self-control hard, I wasn't sick.

Within an hour or so I was in Edinburgh and feeling normal again, then came back by night train, calling in at the Admiralty before reporting at my base. I was away six days all by myself.

Actually, as regards the flying part, an RAF brass hat remarked on landing that it had been 'most unpleasantly rough'!

16 December 1942   HMS *Mercury I*, Haslemere, Surrey

Dearest

Had a marvellous time yesterday. I was superintending some crates being put in the luggage van at a London station when the bottom fell out of one of them and the stuff was scattered on the line. God, what a moment! And I'd just had to draw the station foreman's attention to someone who was taking rather too much interest in my crates.

It's a little nerve-racking this job, you know. You can't relax a second.

17 December 1942   HMS *Mercury I*, Haslemere, Surrey

The Compton village knitting party have made me a superb polo-necked naval sweater because I go to sea. Isn't it sweet?

17 December 1942   HMS *Mercury I*, Haslemere, Surrey

I have tried to give you some idea of what these extraordinary women are like that I'm working with. The first impression that I got of them was that they were peculiarly ugly and very repressed. Last night I nearly cried in my bunk. It was the same as most other nights but I wasn't feeling too well. From after supper until 12.30 or 1 am the conversation was their eternal one – sex.

Over and over again they describe their 'experiences', their friends' experiences, the dirty books they've read, the men they've known. And the married women do it too. If I'd come into this room ignorant of the facts of life I'd have learnt them all by now. I just lie in my little bunk and say nothing.

I try to sleep but their furtive cackles keep me awake.

18 December 1942   The Dykeries, Compton, Guildford, Surrey

Dearest one

Am a little weary if the truth be told. Liverpool is a tiresome trip but there was an amusing occurrence on the station. A little man in civilians and his wife seemed to be fascinated by my gear and when the woman began lifting things and peeking I bristled very visibly. 'Oh,' she said, 'I'm so intrigued. Do tell me where they are going.'

I was just about to answer when the little man said, 'It's all right, my dear. I'm just retired from being C-in-C, Portsmouth Command.' It was Admiral James![1] Even so, I did not say where I was going. I had no intention of falling into that sort of trap.

Liverpool was uninteresting – except that I was gaily tripping up the steps of a naval establishment in the blackout when I found a bayonet an inch from my tummy and a fearsome-looking sailor shouting, 'Halt! Who goes there?' Quite overcome, I stuttered, 'Me friend ... me courier ... Wren ...'

Coming down in the night train I was sitting next to a big bug in the Royal Marines. He had a gorgeous Alsatian puppy, four months old, which spent the night in my arms. Its master told me it had been reared and bred for the purpose of being the RM's mascot and that it was called 'Hannah' after a famous woman who joined the marines and fought in battles with the men. I feel I've had quite an honour.

22 December 1942   HMS *Mercury I*, Haslemere, Surrey

I've had a good insight into the services in this job. It's funny how different they are.

The navy has more gentlemen than the others. An admiral will get into the carriage, sit down quietly and read his paper. Except for his gold braid you'd hardly know he was there.

A major will get in, blow himself out, shout at porters, throw his things into the rack and generally let you know he's there.

---

[1] Admiral Sir William Milburne James, 1881–1973. Commander-in-Chief, Portsmouth, 1939–1942. He was known throughout the navy as 'Bubbles' because when he was a child his grandfather Sir John Millais had painted a portrait of him blowing soap bubbles through a clay pipe. The picture was later bought by the Pears Soap company and reproduced in a famous advertisement.

The RAF vary enormously. Young pilot officers are arrogant and supercilious. Squadron leaders upwards are either extremely pleasant to travel with, considerate and unselfish, or the lords of creation. I've heard it said that the RAF is the most democratic and the navy the most snob service.

It's a curious thing but a naval man will never turn a hair when I, a mere rating, get in. I've been offered lots of cigarettes by admirals and captains – but this is what happened to me at Cardiff. I got the only corner seat I could find and was just taking off my coat when a pip of a young pilot officer lent across and in a high-pitched squeak said, 'Er, if you want the third class it's along the corridor.'

I looked at him calmly and said, 'Thank you, I don't.' Then, who should get in but a very high-up Wren, a chief officer. Delighted, the pilot officer glanced at the businessman sitting opposite him. I felt a little embarrassed. The Wren officer said good morning to me and began to talk to me as if I was her equal! I soon forgot her rank – she was just a charming woman, aged forty to fifty. The pilot officer began to deflate visibly. Then he went along the passage, came back, smirked at me and said, 'The ticket collector's coming round.'

I made no reply but slowly brought out my first class ticket...

26 December 1942   HMS *Mercury I*, Haslemere, Surrey

Dearest

How do you feel this morning? Have you a hangover? Do you feel as low as I do? Thank God Christmas is over.

Yesterday morning I went to early service. Every Wren had an egg for breakfast as a special Christmas treat. Betty, Jane and I then felt so fed up we thought we'd go on a pub crawl. We tried several places and found they weren't opening till 12.30. We installed ourselves by the fire of the Georgian Hotel to wait. We imbibed Pimms No.1 when the bar opened and I felt better after it. After that we made our way back to the quarters for Christmas lunch, all girls together. Small drinks first, so so hearty, everyone striving to keep in good spirits.

Presents were given out, one to each Wren. I got a slightly drippy powder puff with pink satin nob. After the meal and the King's speech we did the washing up for the stewards to give them a holiday. Tea was so exciting. The quarters officer brought in her boyfriend, a Canadian major. The gardener, old Mr Hawkes, came in too. We all sat in a row round the fire and ate cake. I entertained the gardener. He's adorable. He said the Wrens weren't arf ever ser nice.

At 6 Betty, Jane, another girl (called Pat) and I were called for and driven over to Headley to see old friends of Betty's living there. A young woman whose husband is out East and her widowed sister, who are fabulously well off and live in a big luxurious country house with their kids – a really lovely place reeking of big money. The only other guests were fifteen Canadian officers.

I seemed to spend the whole evening changing chairs so as to avoid one after the other. They all came absolutely sozzled. The two hostesses are a couple of Mayfair lassies and have both lived with heaven knows how many men. They soon became as tight as their male guests and it developed into a petting session.

Betty vaguely drummed out dance music in the corner. Pat and mine hostesses were oblivious on various sofas. Jane (awfully attractive and charming to a degree) and I told each other how we liked the RAF. Eventually the car came to take us home. We arrived at the quarters. The key was under the mat but as they'd bolted the door inside we couldn't get in. We had a happy quarter of an hour in the freezing cold trying to wake the petty officer by throwing pebbles at her window.

This was Christmas 1942. I hope yours was more fun.

29 December 1942   The Dykeries, Compton, Guildford, Surrey

Yesterday Jane and I skipped church parade by putting on our macks, which are like ordinary civvie ones, and running for our lives out of the back door and through the vegetable garden to a by-road. It's an asset to have gone to boarding school – one knows all the tricks!

Jane, Betty and I then did the quite unforgivable thing. We imbibed gin and lime out of our tooth mugs in the cabin. Booze in the bedroom!

Had we been caught I dread to think of the consequences.

11 January 1943   HMS *Mercury I*, Haslemere, Surrey

Poor Jane had an awful trip the other day. She had to stand for ten hours – Euston to Glasgow – squashed between drunk soldiers.

Our cabin is ruined as we were three together, all great friends, Betty, Jane and I, and now we've been invaded by writers, some of whom get into bed with all their clothes on. The colour of the underclothes of the girl in the next bunk to me would have to be seen to be believed. And she held quite a good secretarial job before the war. I complained of feeling a little cold in bed the other night and she said, 'Well, why on earth do you undress completely before you put on your pyjamas?'

Betty promptly gave my mattress a large poke from her bunk under mine and I nearly fell out of bed.

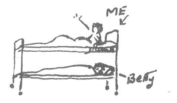

20 January 1943   The Dykeries, Compton, Guildford, Surrey

Have I ever told you about my pals? I'm lucky as they're absolutely grand.

Betty is twenty-five, tiny, rather gingery haired, a hundred per cent Irish (like me) and sort of rounded. She is as bright as a button and definitely attractive. Her father is a colonel in the Scottish Borderers and she's had quite a gay time around Hong Kong and Cairo pre-war.

Jane is one of the most remarkable women I have ever met. She's very thin, very dark, with deep-set eyes and 'careless' hair and is actually awfully hard to describe. She's very quiet until you know her, then she's vivacity itself with a sense of humour that matches Betty's and mine. But the most remarkable thing about her is the youth that she radiates. We thought she was about twenty-eight. People at home said not a day over twenty-five.

Her actual age is forty and I still cannot believe it. She's the youngest woman in spirit I've ever met and in addition she's brilliantly intelligent. When quite young she married a naval officer and was very happy. After some years he died and Jane became a widow. She's travelled and knocked about a lot. Four years ago she married again, a big, comfortable, kindly, humorous creature. She can't be very happy with him or she wouldn't have come in the service.

I'd love you to meet her as I know you'd like her enormously. There's breeding in every line of her face.

22 January 1943   The Dykeries, Compton, Guildford, Surrey

We had a very fair Ensa show at quarters last week, one of the best I've seen, I think. There was an amazingly versatile actor who conjured, sang arias, told some excellent yarns and did a clever ventriloquist act and a lot of odd turns.

He kept making flirtatious remarks at a prim and staid Wren officer in the front row, which delighted the rows of little Wren ratings more than anything.

26 January 1943   The Dykeries, Compton, Guildford, Surrey

… It's not the work I mind, it's what you come back to when you're dead beat. You crawl up the hill to the quarters – and they're such lovely quarters, a big old house in pleasant grounds – and you open the heavy old door and step into the large panelled hall. Somehow the general turmoil is utterly depressing. The wireless is blaring jazz from the recreation room. The tinny gramophone is blaring a different tune from the galley. There is the noise of shuffling feet – stewards dancing together, girls desperately seeking a little 'gaiety'. Amazingly plain women are walking about. 'Hullo, Bolster, had a good trip?' 'What did you do with yourself in Liverpool?' One knows only too well what most of *them* do.

You write your name in the book to show that you are in, then you slowly go upstairs and along the long passage to the last door on the right. Your own bunk is the top one in the far corner, by the window. The room seems full of people. 'Hullo, just back from a job?' (Surely that's obvious.) All you want is sleep, deep, blessed sleep. But you mustn't think of that yet – you couldn't sleep in the daytime here. No, somehow you must keep going till lights out. A bath! The prospect of solitude and blessed comfort. Comfort, yes, but not solitude. In the next cubicle is a girl who chats away. You lie there, drowsy in the steam, and wish to heaven she'd stop. But she only works four hours a day and doesn't understand.

You get dressed in clean clothes and wander downstairs. Jane is sitting in the alcove sewing, her mouth full of pins. She waves and pulls up a chair for you. There's something comforting about Jane: I'm sure men must love her. She says, 'Betty's gone to Manchester!' We both laugh, as Betty attracts the dirty jobs like a magnet and it's become a byword.

And then the gong goes. Immediately there's a mad rush for the mess room. A crowd mills round the teapot, everyone scrambling for places. You and Jane take what's left. It's better that way. Why fight when you can get sufficient by waiting? It's good food, better than civilians could imagine, but eaten under what conditions – noise and scramble and pushing and grabbing.

You are doubtless sitting opposite a courier who is like a pig in face and body. Or it may be the one with whiskers and protruding teeth. Or the parson's wife with the neck of her shirt collar indescribably black or that ex-barmaid whose husband is a naval officer and whose blonded frizz and hideously overdeveloped chest takes away one's appetite.

14 February 1943   HMS *Mercury I*, Haslemere, Surrey

Dearest

It's extraordinary. I have only to walk into the recreation room with my pen, ink and a couple of airgraph forms for the chorus to start. 'More airgraphs, Maureen!' 'How many is that this week?' 'Wasting *more* paper?' 'Does he ever read them?' 'My dear, it's someone who's been away two years.' 'Two years! The girl's barmy.' 'I'm hanged if I'd bother with anyone after six months.' 'Do you ever get an answer?'

They really do think I'm barmy. Do you?

16 February 1943   HMS *Mercury I*, Haslemere, Surrey

Dearest

Suppose you were a fly on the wall in our recreation room tonight this is what you'd hear:

'Did you go by the 10.35 or 11.45?'
'When I was coming back from Scapa . . .'
'How much was bed and breakfast at Barrow-in-Furness?'
'Did you queue in Edinburgh for the midnight?'
'Was it rough going over to Londonderry?'
'Did Commander so-and-so offer you a meal?'
'If I get another day job I'll scream.'
'Mona's been to Manchester three times this week.'
'What time is the first train to Hull in the morning?'
'How many nights was Jane away?'
'My dear, the RTO at Dundee is a poppet!'
'I'd adore a job to Plymouth.'
'Alex hasn't yet done that Newcastle trip.'
'You should have seen what I spent the night with. It snored like a pig and shook the carriage.'
'Of course I lost my ticket at Crewe.'
'Nutt had to stand the whole way to Carlisle.'
'The Wrennery at Cardiff positively reeks.'
'Lieutenant C is always so *rude*.'
'The porters ran a mile, my dear.'
'Transport was half an hour late.'
'How I *loathe* that place.'

I used to be rather impressed when I was new. Now that I'm a walking Bradshaw I'm impressed no longer!

16 February 1943   HMS *Mercury I*, Haslemere, Surrey

Dearest Eric

I've discovered a brand new technique. Waterloo has a pukka post office so instead of storing up airgraphs till I have time to post them in the village I can now do it while setting forth on jobs. I am sitting before the fire in quarters. The wireless can be vaguely heard from the galley. 'Who's taking you home tonight?' Remember how they used to play that after every dance in 1940?

Today is Saturday. Since this time last Tuesday I have been to Leatherhead, Glasgow, Greenock, Tottenham and Witley. I don't think that's bad, do you? And now, having just come in, I find I'm duty courier again. Please God, let me have a night in bed tonight.

Later. Have had an amusing time this evening designing glamorous hair styles for the little stewards who're going out tonight with their Canadian Tommies. They're all so excited with their new-found beauty and are longing to see if the boyfriends notice anything. 'Ow, Maureen, make me beautiful too!'

Our cabins are called after ships and so far I've been in HMS *Dolphin, Saladin* and *Indomitable*. Our present one is unnamed so far. As it is by far the gayest (and noisiest) we're going to call it HMS *Hilarious*.

2 March 1943   Glasgow

Dearest Eric

I couldn't let 2 March go by without writing to you, especially as I've been thinking so much about you today. Three years since we met, my love! Three whole years – and what a marvellous day that was. I'll never forget any detail of it – ever.

I'm writing this in the Naval Club at Glasgow. It's nice and quiet in here, a pleasant refuge from trains and noisy cities. One can get superb sausages and chips too. It's been a busy day but it all began last night really. I'd had my supper and settled down for an evening's sewing when suddenly I had to rush off within a quarter of an hour of the train's departure.

I had to be in Greenock by this morning. Hurtled across London in service transport. Missed train by five minutes at Euston. Choice of ghastly journey with four changes in the middle of the night or waiting till next morning and being late on the job. Nothing for it but to conscientiously decide to do the filthy journey.

The chief petty officer at the railway transport office, however, is a poppet and decided otherwise – said it wasn't a fit journey for any girl. He called a car and said I was to be driven at top speed to King's Cross to catch the night train to Edinburgh and get to Glasgow that way.

It was a most exciting ride. We tore through the black-out and I scarcely dared breathe for fear we shouldn't make it. I leapt into the train as it was going.

I sought out the guard, announced who I was and asked him to get me a seat. The train was packed to the doors. All first class compartments were jammed full. The only seat he could manage for me was in third class – and how!

Dearest, how can I describe to you the sordidness? I sat bolt upright and sleepless for eleven hours, tightly wedged between a sailor lad and a *passée* prostitute of forty something whose make up was so caked it began to peel off in layers towards morning. Opposite me was one of those amazing females – stout, Eton-cropped, tight-lipped, bulging out of her Waaf uniform.

Next to her was a stout party of the fishwife variety, who went to pay a penny about every twenty minutes with tedious regularity. The other occupants were insignificant.

In the next compartment a baby howled and howled. The Waaf opposite me was blessed with legs like barrage balloons. When I came back from a wash there she was, feigning sleep, with her repulsive limbs and feet on my seat. I firmly lifted them up and put them on the floor. She soon awoke. 'Oh,' she said, 'I do think you might let me leave my feet up.' I asked her where she thought I was going to sit.

This hell continued till 9 am. There was, however, the most wonderful sunrise to be seen over the sea going from Berwick to Edinburgh, which was something for my aching eyes to rest on.

On arrival in Edinburgh had two minutes in which to run for my Glasgow train. No hope of a bite to eat. Arrival at Glasgow entailed another dash by taxi to a different station and a run and a leap into the train. At least I made it – in the only possible way. I got to Greenock this morning and am rather proud of it.

Greenock usually provides a pleasant hour or so. I had a frantic time leaping from drifter to drifter with a lieutenant-commander, in search of all sorts of things, terrified of falling into the sea and still more terrified of showing that I was afraid of doing same. Much

Perhaps we'll be together March 2nd 1944 ..... !
Lots & Lots of Love,
dearest
Noreen.
We're sposed to wear awfull "dark Knickers close to the knee," which we call BLACKOUTS!
I'm not often guilty!

interest in my gambollings was shown by groups of sailors standing around. I've had quite a lot of practice in this business of leaping from boat to boat.

My pals there are the fishermen and old tars who sail the little drifters. I sat happily chatting to them for half an hour or so today while the boat swayed up and down. I had to slip my chin strap down for fear my hat would blow away. I made a point of looking up my old friend the skipper who took me out to sea last November. I was pleased to note that my seaman's sweater is the same as they all wear.

I'm vilely tired. Last night really was the end so I've pulled strings and got someone turfed out of a sleeper for my benefit. I've got to pay out of my own money but it's worth it.

7 March 1943   HMS *Mercury I*, Haslemere, Surrey

Since Monday evening I've been to Edinburgh, Glasgow, Greenock, Plymouth and Devonport. The last trip was really most pleasant. I enjoyed it a lot. The weather was too lovely to be true. I left London about 3 pm by an express, chattered French most of the way with a Belgian and ate chocolates offered by a business man (first I'd consumed for months and months!).

A Wren second officer was also in the carriage, a mature and pleasant woman of doubtful origin and background. She wasn't in the least 'officerish' in her attitude to a mere rating and was most chatty.

I nearly died of suppressed laughter as an elderly man friend of hers got in and at about 5 o'clock pulled out a whisky bottle. 'Have a swig with me, Bessie,' he said to her. 'No thank you,' she replied rather stiffly and with the dignity becoming her rank.

'Aw, come on, Bessie. 'Tisn't like *you* to refuse a good old swig with a pal, is it now?' She went purple with embarrassment. I felt so sorry for her. Moral: Be sure your sins will find you out.

Arrived at Plymouth at 9 pm and was met by RN transport. What a ride! My driver (a civilian) had definitely been having some fun. 'Come along, my little angel, you come sit by me. There, my darling. You're more my cup of tea than the one who came last night. She weren't no armful of cuddle like you, my love.'

This went on till we reached our destination. I don't know where we went. We drove on through the night, past ghoulish ruined shapes set against the starry sky, arriving at a place where there were men with guns and you had to give a password. It was most exciting. I then found myself in a room full of sailors, playing the piano and playing cards. I was regaled with a drink and supper and pressed to join in some weird card game I didn't in the least understand. Sailors are wonderful people. I really think the ordinary rating is the kindest and most open-hearted in the world.

One of them went and phoned all the Wren quarters in Plymouth till he found Susan Creasey, an old school pal of mine. At last I set forth again into the night with my driver and eventually drew up before the quarters where Susan was.

Suddenly an amazing apparition ran out of the front door in dressing gown, curlers and face cream. 'Are you the strange Wren who's coming for the night? Do come in. You're in our cabin.' She was very kind. Then Susan rescued me and I got straight into the bath while she sat on the floor and talked to me. I was awfully glad to see her – as big and blonde as ever. Very clever, too. She's doing intelligence.

I spent the night in a room with girls who are all in boats' crews. They man small boats and dress in bell bottoms and lanyards. But, dearest, you should see their muscles! Never, never will I go in boats' crews.

Susan and I breakfasted early, then I went with her by bus to her work about thirty minutes away. It was the most beautiful morning – a faint mist, sun, spring and tremendously exhilarating air. We parted and I went up to Plymouth Hoe. Plymouth Hoe where Drake played bowls. I'd been longing to go to Plymouth and wasn't disappointed. Anything more lovely than the harbour under the sunlight couldn't be imagined.

I stood under Drake's statue and loved everything in sight. But, my dearest, the bomb damage! Many say that it's the worst in the country. It's absolutely devastating and horrified me right to the depths. I'd thought that nothing could be worse than Liverpool but this was and there was something so frantically tragic about it. It really shook me.[1]

Back to London by midday train. A very nasty old wing commander sitting next to me tried to make me go for a weekend with him. 'Love you to meet the squadron. Yes, rather!' I made it more than plain that I had a travelling job and could not make private arrangements. Dirty old man! A pity for him it was me and not one of the others. And so back to quarters to find I'm second on the list.

Wonder where I'll go today.

21 March 1943   The Dykeries, Compton, Guildford, Surrey

Dearest

Am home recuperating after a somewhat gruelling three weeks of non-stop travelling. My last trip was to Newcastle. In the morning I went to the railway transport officer at King's Cross and said, 'I'm a courier and I'm travelling on the 3.50. Can you tell me what time the train gets in the station so that I can get a good seat?' 'Oh,' he said, 'courier! You'll want a compartment reserved for you. Quite easily done.'

Now we are not entitled to this unless carrying frightfully secret stuff on our persons and even then very seldom. However, I sort of said, 'Oh ... um ... ah,' and was whisked off by the RTO – a Scots Guardsman. Before I knew where I was I had a compartment reserved for me.

I came back at 3.30 and gave orders for my one hundredweight crate to be put in my compartment. They measured it and found it too wide so it had to go in the van.

I was in a nice pickle then. I couldn't very well keep my compartment as my gear wasn't with me and all other first class seats had gone. There was nothing for it but to bluff. I went and sat in the compartment, which was plastered with notices saying 'Admiralty Courier', 'Not for Public Use'. I made myself comfortable and strewed my things around.

---

[1] The centre of Plymouth was gutted in a two-night blitz on 20 and 21 March 1941 and the city suffered further heavy raids in the last week of April.

Meanwhile all sorts of majors and colonels were stamping up and down the corridor trying to find seats. They saw the notices on my windows, looked in and seeing just a little Wren sitting there obviously thought they could come in too. To each one that tried it I said, 'I'm sorry. This is not for public use.' They went away looking *furious*!

I began to enjoy myself enormously. The guard came along to assure me my gear would be OK in his loving care, the assistant station master paid me a visit to see if I was all right and then the seat attendant came to see if I needed anything. I told him that as the train was so full and I wasn't carrying anything on my person I didn't mind if he put some people in with me.

He went away after profusely thanking me and soon returned with a very grand person. Did I mind if Lady so-and-so came in with me? I very graciously said, 'No, no, not a bit,' and the aristocracy sat itself down opposite me. The seat attendant then produced a commander RN, a colonel, a flight lieutenant and a major – impressing on them how privileged they were. At the end each thanked me warmly for my kindness in letting them join me.

I laughed like a drain.

24 March 1943   HMS *Mercury I*, Haslemere, Surrey

Dearest

It's a relief to have you to write to, to restore my sense of balance and proportion. The day before yesterday I came back from my weekend just in time for a couriers meeting with our Wren CO. Within ten minutes it had developed into the most despicable cat fight, with everyone getting in sly digs at everyone else. I can't tell you how awful it was.

Now, ever since, there's been a first class courier fight going on. Half of them are not on speaking terms with the other half – there are about six different sides. One of them came hissing up to me yesterday and in grim and abusive language accused me of something I've never done.

I was afraid she was going to scratch me.

Dearest, you really are a pet! So you think I ought to be an officer do you? There's a lot I must explain.

Your knowledge of the women's services is limited to the WAAF: mine now covers all three. The ATS and WAAF are similar – run on exactly the same lines. Really only the colour of the uniform is different. Anyone can get into either, no matter from what walk of life she comes.

The WRNS, however, hardly resembles them at all. It is less than a third of their size, the need for large numbers not being there. The navy, as the senior service, claimed the right to pick and choose its female members with care and discretion.

Every Wren has had to give three references and undergo a lot of checking up on before acceptance. Hundreds are turned down. Nine out of ten Waafs that I've met travelling have told me they failed for the Wrens.

The service, being relatively small, needs fewer officers than the other services. This means that we do not have to resort to putting young things aged nineteen or so in for commissions as the ATS and WAAF do. Instead, only experienced women of suitable age are given the responsibility – and it's *so* much better like that. Only in the most exceptional cases can a girl get any sort of commission under twenty-five, except in coding, when she must be twenty-one. It does mean that the average Wren has much more respect for her officers than the average Waaf or ATS girl.

My CO is a good forty, my quarters officer not a day under thirty-five. Both nice women who are experienced and capable – and we look up to them.

A Waaf at Ashley House (where I stay in London) told me the other day that her officer was nineteen – five years younger than herself – and she resented taking orders from her.

Because the navy makes a point of having older women as officers it gives them a great deal of responsibility. To be a Wren officer is therefore not a thing to be sought after for anyone under twenty-eight. It means loneliness and damn hard work and worry.

The Wren officer is a most dignified person to meet in a train or socially. She is usually very charming – aloof, though – and you never forget she is an officer in the senior service. The bluejacket is *terrified* of her and naval officers below the rank of captain run a mile. Admirals and such admire them and their very excellent work.

It's no uplift socially to take a commission in the Wrens as it is in the ATS and WAAF as the Wren rating is socially on a par with the latter's officer – and pretty well as her own officers.

Moreover, all the swank jobs in the Wrens – boats' crews, motor transport, dispatch riders, couriers – have no promotion at all.

The difficulty is to find girls who *want* a commission. You've got to have private means and, frankly, the only assets are the most glamorous of all the women's service uniforms and a bedroom to yourself.

Am I clear?

I pray you will never see me in a tricorne, even in imagination. The saucy little sailor cap suits me *so* much better!

15 April 1943   HMS *Mercury I*, Haslemere, Surrey

On Monday I went on a job to Woolwich and crossed the Thames by ferry. I can't help thinking how nice it would be to be a seafaring Wren. To wear bell bottoms just like the sailors and a lanyard and sail harbour boats and go out to big ships with their crews, mails and visitors. I'd get a bed every night (heavenly thought) and I'd be in the open air (relief after interminable hours in stuffy trains). There are a picked lot doing it and the call of the sea is tempting.

It's tough work but I wouldn't let it make *me* tough. I haven't let couriering make me tough! I've not got whiskers, beefy legs and arms, buck teeth or straight hair or a large tum or square-cut nails or a skin like an orange peel.

Would you love me if I had?

20 April 1943   HMS *Mercury I*, Haslemere, Surrey

I'm awaiting at the moment the form of application for a draft and change of category. It'll take ages to go through. The navy is awfully slow over things like that. Jane is getting a commission, Betty is going into regulating and life at Haslemere without them is not to be considered for a moment.

Do you know that those other hags are so furiously resentful of Jane's going up for a commission that they refuse to address one word to her? Can you imagine what it's like living in such an atmosphere of petty jealousy and spite? They even went in a semihysterical body to the officer and complained about 'that Jane Moore going to OCTU'. They were told to mind their own business.

Only Betty and Jane know I'm going. Betty and I are naturally included in Jane's unpopularity and we are referred to as 'that Moore', 'that Bolster' and 'that Comyn' by the other couriers.

22 April 1943   HMS *Mercury I*, Haslemere, Surrey

Dearest Eric

Our wireless is playing a Johann Strauss waltz – 'A Thousand and One Nights'. I can hardly bear it. What I would give to dance with you again, to go to a big pukka dance, to wear my full crinoline with bare shoulders, and enormous skirt of black and pink lace and a flower in my hair.

I'm tired of wearing blue serge and collars and ties. I want to go all glamorous.

Last night I signed my fate on the dotted line – on the form of application for change of category. I've no regrets.

Today I took it up to Lieutenant-Commander Jolly, my boss. He was very nice. He said he quite understood, that I'd done an excellent job of work and that he would be pleased to recommend me for boats' crews. I explained that I was too young to go without so much sleep and he quite agreed.

I know I've done the right thing.

Love,
Maureen.

85

28 April 1943   Llandudno

You'll never guess where I'm writing to you from. I'm sitting up in bed in an ATSery in Llandudno in North Wales. It's a boarding house taken over and I'm the army's guest for the night. An enormous sergeant-major received me.

So this is life in the ATS... I'm very pleased to have a taste of it. This is a tiny attic room lit by a skylight only. The wallpaper is green – stained and faded in places and positively peeling off in strips. A filthy-dirty orange curtain across the corner does for a cupboard. Here and there are khaki ties, stockings and oddments lying about. There's a smell of stale sweat. The lino on the floor is all cracked and curling up. The mirror is cracked too and spotted. The mantelpiece is thick with dust and in the grate is a repulsive collection of matches, dirty hair ribbons, paper and hair combings. I think the only clean part of the room is my bed linen.

There's only one other bed in here – belonging to a lass from Birkenhead. She's sitting up, cross-legged, in her blue and white striped flannel pyjamas, polishing her buttons. She's very grubby but has a heart of gold. Calls me 'duck' and 'luv'.

I shall have to give up in a minute. There's a regular party going on in here. I'm the first Wren most of them have ever talked to and I'm a sort of encyclopaedia. There's one that's come in in her pyjamas, hat and topcoat, swinging a sponge bag and smoking a cigarette in a long holder, her glasses on the end of her nose. I really don't think she's conscious of her appearance.

I wish they'd go to bed. It's long after eleven. It's all very hearty and ever such fun – but I'm tired...

30 April 1943   HMS *Mercury I*, Haslemere, Surrey

Do you remember my telling you some weeks back how I went to Oldham to get something to take to a ship somewhere in the British Isles and how I went aboard in the dead of night and we tore open the crates on deck by the light of the moon and my torch? They were Norwegians and perfectly charming and were awaiting my arrival before they could sail.

I've now heard they've been lost with all hands. It's shaken me to the core. I was the last woman they ever saw.

I can remember the faces of those men as clearly as daylight.

7 May 1943 HMS *Mercury I*, Haslemere, Surrey

I'm giving this job up because:

1. I've now done it for six months and by the time I get a draft it will be eight or nine months. That is long enough for any normal person to be continually going without sleep or food and living on buns and tea. I really am now beginning to feel tired out and I need a change.

2. I definitely can't afford it. I'm the only one without private means and through some mistake I was the only one who wasn't told that they liked you to have money of your own.

3. Haslemere is the most dead and alive hole you could ever wish for. No dances, no fun, nothing. It feels like the forestry department, not the WRNS.

4. I do want a little time off occasionally.

5. I have visited enough other Wrenneries all over the country to see that I am particularly unlucky in my work mates.

6. I want to go by the sea.

7. The summer in this job is grim hell. Nothing attracts heat like a railway carriage and trains are crowded out with workers on holiday.

8. I've now been all over the country from Devon to Scapa Flow, from Liverpool to Chatham. I've been to practically all the places I want to go to and I now feel that I want to settle down in a port.

9. One doesn't use one's brain, only common sense, and I think when you're young that's bad. I want a job where I can be active yet use my brain, or else it will decay and go woolly.

Still, I'll never regret being a courier. It was an honour to be chosen and it's been an incomparable experience. I wouldn't *not* have done it for anything in the world.

10 May 1943   The Dykeries, Compton, Guildford, Surrey

Dearest

Adventure is all very well but one can have too much of it at one go. I doubt if you've ever known physical hardship such as I've been experiencing! Last Tuesday week I left on a rather trying trip to Chelmsford and Llandudno. Was back on Thursday night. On Friday night I went up on the night train to Edinburgh, which meant of course no sleep. Back on Sunday very tired indeed. On Monday I was sent up to Rochdale to get several hundredweight to take to Plymouth (a nasty job). Still feeling very tired I got into the midnight to Manchester – usual thing, couldn't sleep. Arrived 4.30 am and made my way out to Rochdale. Long walk to the factory and by the time I'd got there was literally in a state of complete exhaustion. I'd never been like that before. I could hardly hold up my head and it was as much as I could do to mumble a few words. I'm sure I'd have fainted if they hadn't put me to bed at once.

They *were* kind, those North-country factory people. I was put in the loft above the boiler room as that was the only warm place. It was filthy dirty and I strongly suspected rats. The heat came through in waves but I was past caring – it was somewhere for me to lay my head. Puzzled but kindly workmen tucked me up: they'd never had a Wren go to sleep in their loft before!

I slept soundly for a few hours and was then awoken to be told I was not to go to Plymouth but to Scapa Flow. I just blinked. Scapa! There was I ready only for a journey to the sunny south being sent to the frozen north! I'd only got my light mack and, mercifully, my rug, no greatcoat – let alone my duffle coat – no change of shirt, not enough money, no hair or clothes brush or other necessities for a week's non-stop travelling. *Screamingly* funny joke.

Wandered down to Rochdale and got some lunch. I could hardly walk owing to a large blister on my heel and, as it was early closing, the chemists were all shut. I had a trying afternoon being fixed up with warrants to Scapa and having to go to another factory to have them stamped.

Left Rochdale about 7 in a lorry with a working party, who got my stuff into the train. I treated them to tea and penny buns in the canteen. An hour's run to Crewe, then an hour's wait on the station. Picked up a most amiable if quaint WAAF officer who was also going to Inverness. By some amazing stroke of luck we got a compartment to ourselves and settled down. Suddenly there was an awful noise. We looked out into the corridor. There was a large swarm of Indian soldiers pouring into all the first class compartments. We quickly thrust something on each seat and said they were all taken.

Do you know, Eric, I cannot describe to you the hell of those night trains. I lay there again utterly sleepless through the night. It was completely unheated. The cold was intense and we both had dreadful bouts of shivering. The further north we got the worse it was. My feet and toes were numb. There was only cold water to wash in.

At Inverness we made for the station hotel where we imbibed hot coffee and gradually thawed. My journey to Thurso, despite the fact I'd had three hours' sleep in fifty-six, was very nice. I had grand people in the carriage, with whom I lunched.

Reached Thurso about 19.30 and went to the Wren transit house where I'm now an old friend. Had meal, bath and bed – then of all horrors had to arise at 7 as a draft of 45 Wrens had come off the night train and needed breakfast. Lord, what chaos! Nothing for it but to put on an apron and help in the galley. I did most of the washing up, then was called for in the duty officer's car and driven to the boat.

The 45 Wrens were already aboard, all very excited and giggling and trying to get off with the sailors. I found two congenial spirits and we sat on a sort of chest affair on deck. It was fairly choppy with sunshine but stormy clouds were coming. The water was deep blue and the isles were looking as lovely as usual.

In half an hour the little Wrens were happy and giggling no longer. It was impossible to get into the saloon – it was full of Wrens and suitcases and were some of them *ill*! I was busy doling out Rennie tablets. I didn't feel a twinge myself but suffered hell from the cold. The gale went right through my thin mack to my body till I was stiff and numb. My lips became salty and my hair wild. Still, as I wasn't sick I'm not grumbling.

There was the usual fun of the Wren courier having a drifter come out specially for her while naval officers and ratings piled into the other ones. They were, as always, perfectly sweet to me when I arrived. I was given cups of tea and work stopped generally. I then crossed the Flow with my old friend Joe in his drifter. He's a darling. His face is lined by years of seafaring, his eyes are bright blue and he wears a filthy old blue sweater. We had a nice two-hour run with me in the wheel room.

Late evening found me at Hatston Royal Naval Air Station – at my favourite Wrens quarters. I was in a state of such complete exhaustion the sister said I must not go back next day. Bed very very early, having met all the friends I made up there before and having phoned my cousin in the flagship.[1] I had a long long sleep and arose next morning feeling grand. The air up there is the best tonic I know of. It was one of the happiest days I've had since I joined the Wrens.

I went down to Kirkwall with some friends (*lovely* Kirkwall) and had coffee and bought some tweed and lots and lots of eggs for Mummy.

After lunch I had a good rest. By the evening I was feeling so restored in strength that I succumbed to temptation and went to the most wonderful Fleet Air Arm all ranks dance – really terrific. Those men have so little time and opportunity for a spree that when they do get one they throw all they've got into it. It's a very long time since I've had an evening like that.

Next morning I wandered down to the air ferry house. The first thing I was told was that the weather was so bad that no planes had come up from Scotland, nor had any been allowed from the Orkneys. They were, however, letting an aircraft go to Inverness and I could travel on that!

I struggled through the gale into the plane and was given the seat by the wireless operator in front. I was the only woman aboard. All I can tell you, dearest, is that I was very ill. We rolled about the sky through snowstorms and what have you in one of the most danger-ous parts of the world for sailing and flying. My face became as white as a sheet and I thought I'd faint. I had to pull myself together. The pilot kept looking round and offering me cigarettes but I couldn't make him hear I didn't smoke.

When we landed I had to be half lifted out. By the luck of Mike there was a sick bay orderly in the plane and he and a petty officer more or less carried me into the transport. At Inverness they got me into the canteen and filled me with cups of tea and I came round eventually. They were *so* sweet – really couldn't have been kinder.

[1] Paymaster Commander Richard Mann Bolster RN, who was serving in HMS *Duke of York*. He was awarded the OBE for his part in the battle of North Cape on 26 December 1943, when the German battlecruiser *Scharnhorst* was sunk. An account he wrote of the action is held by the Museum's Department of Documents.

Feeling extremely weak, I clambered into the London train at 4.20 pm. Outside a blizzard was raging. Snow and sleet alternately beat against the windows. Inside it was again unheated. We were an elderly member of the Ministry of Aircraft Production, an army officer's wife (camp follower) and a charming commander RN. We stamped our feet, huddled ourselves up, clapped our hands – and soon became numb. Before long I lost the feel of my fingers. The army officer's wife tried to control tears of cold creeping down her cheeks. We attempted to laugh it all off but it really became more than a joke.

As we began to settle down for the night the commander suddenly produced out of his case a large white sweater, a pair of flannel slacks and two large pairs of woolly socks in which he proceeded to dress me. Was I grateful! But even with these, cold – intense cold – made sleep impossible. We sat there through the night really jibbering with cold, chatting at intervals. I made my way home next morning (yesterday) and found Mummy in bed with neuritis in her arm, so I concocted some lunch, then went to bed and stayed there till this morning.

Now I'm ready to go out again. God!

Love —
gallows of it —
from
Maureen.

x ooo x & x ooo x
x o x
O x o x o

27 May 1943   HMS *Mercury I*, Haslemere, Surrey

The Duchess of Kent[1] came and inspected us today. She was three-quarters of an hour late, so it meant that we had to stand in the scorching sun for two hours – and most of us got splitting headaches.

I was made a line leader. Having only done squad twice since I left training depot I was petrified that I'd do the wrong thing and disgrace the WRNS. I was expecting her to be very tall and glamorous. She was shorter than me – quite sweet-faced with a lovely speaking voice – but looked really just like any other Wren officer. The captain accompanied her, followed by a trail of Wren officers and various naval highlights.

It was extremely tedious.

19 June 1943   The Dykeries, Compton, Guildford, Surrey

I got home straight from a Glasgow-Greenock trip. I had to train a new courier, a compliment I could well have done without as couriering is strictly a lone wolf business. Her name is Eileen. She's twenty-four, very religious and worthy, and wears her straight black hair dragged off her face into a screwy little bun at the back.

The whole time she kept saying, 'Ow, Maureen, isn't it beeeauuutiful?' We had a reserved compartment on the night express as we had secret gear. About 5 am, after a completely sleepless night and feeling like the wrath of God, I was aroused from my state of coma by the sound of a thin quavery voice chanting, 'Bonnie Scotland, oh bonnie bonnie Scotland.'

I opened one eye and there she was, peering behind the curtain, singing away with excitement at her first glimpse of Scotland. That *had* to stop!

We reached Glasgow at 7 am. I sent her to get a porter. She failed, so I went myself. The next train to Greenock left at 7.15. She said, 'Aw, Maureen, I can't go any further without breakfast. I shall faint.' (She'd had an enormous and solid meat pie about 3.30 am.)

I told her that if she was going to be a courier she must learn that hunger must be endured. She trailed miserably after me into the Greenock train and hummed 'Roamin' in the gloamin'' the whole

[1] Princess Marina, Commandant/Chief Commandant of the WRNS, 1940–1968.

way out. On arrival I phoned for transport from the station. While we were waiting for it she went to pay a penny. A few minutes later she came back soaking. When she pulled the plug the contents of the water tank surged out on top of her! I felt terribly sorry for her but I couldn't help laughing to myself.

Then occurred something which infuriated me. Along came an MT driver in a car to collect us and the gear. I was just getting in when out of the station swept a large and portly Chief Wren (three stripes) and announced that she would take the car.

I said, 'Well ma'am, I would just like to point out that I'm a courier and this gear is most urgently needed in the dockyard.'

She replied, 'I don't care what sort of Wren you are,' and (to the driver), 'Drive off.'

She couldn't have been more insulting.

9 July 1943   HMS *Mercury I*, Haslemere, Surrey

I went to a factory outside London yesterday and collected gear for Witley and Havant. It was an easy though tiring job. I was standing outside Paddington waiting for a taxi when up came a tottery old Cockney woman, who slapped me on my thigh and said:

'That's wot oi loike ter see. Don't cher look nice in yer little skirt.'

(Me) 'Oh?'

'Yeah, none of them 'orrid trousers. Never see wimen nowadays, always them creetures in pants. Yer don't *like* 'em, do yer?'

(Me) 'Er, no, I haven't got any.'

'That's right, dear. You keep yer skirt on and the fellers will love yer. He, he, he.'

And off she hobbled. I rather liked her.

13 July 1943   HMS *Mercury I*, Haslemere, Surrey

Do you know what a woman said to me in the train yesterday? At Bristol five elderly women got in, all going on the spree – and all grumbling about everyone else travelling when they're asked not to by the government.

The worst grumbler, a nasty old b, sat opposite me. She fixed her stony glare on me for a few minutes, then barked out, 'You don't look as if you do any hard work, my girl. Just *what* are you doing for the war?' (My Wren hat was in the rack.)

I was a bit took aback, like, but I recovered and said quietly, 'Absolutely nothing,' (pause) 'that I can tell you anything about.'

Silence ensued and I went on reading.

16 July 1943   HMS *Mercury I*, Haslemere, Surrey

When you think, for a moment, of what life means now – war raging over the world, millions, yes millions, being killed on battle fronts, in the air, on and below the sea and not least in air raids, everyone separated from those they love, millions starving or slave-driven, practically everyone worried about something or someone as never before – it seems such an impossible thing to hope that two ordinary young things, terribly in love, could ever get together again.

And yet, frightened though I am for your safety, I know that you were meant for me and I for you. So I feel that we *will* come together – we must – it could scarcely be otherwise. But I can hardly dare to think about it because it's too much to hope for, it's everything in life and I've done nothing to deserve it.

Why do some people's lives go so smoothly? They meet and fall in love like us but they don't know the ghastly complication of years of separation, with their deep loneliness and longing and hoping.

Perhaps it's their loss, perhaps we'll have such tremendous happiness that it was almost worth the separation. But whether anything could atone for three whole years of youth spent thus, I don't know.

Gallows, Tows, Oceans → oodles of love

FROM
ИƎƎЯUAM

x x x x x x x x x x x x x x
(multiply by 100).
o o o o o o o o o o o o o o

(if you want to find out who this letter is from my love, just hold it to a 'mirror'! The secret will then out!)

21 July 1943   HMS *Mercury I*, Haslemere, Surrey

The first officer went to Pompey yesterday and came back with an offer for me. Sixteen Wrens are being picked for a special course that's never been done before – on engine maintenance and other technicalities. It you pass you go into a specialised job in boats' crews and promotion after is quite quick (if you want it). If I don't do this I'd have to go on waiting months and then go in as general stooge with a boat hook. So, dearest, I have said I will be very pleased to be one of the first sixteen.

The course will be done at Portsmouth. I'm a little afraid that I'll *never* understand the workings of the engines.

29 July 1943   HMS *Mercury I*, Haslemere, Surrey

Lordy, it's hot. I'm duty courier, it's Bank Holiday weekend and the enormous crowds travelling have to be seen to be believed. Last Friday afternoon two thousand got left behind at Waterloo. One couldn't even get on at King's Cross. As for hotel accommodation in the west and south, there just isn't any. Yesterday at Waterloo there was a fantastic queue for a West Country train standing six deep and reaching out of the station.

The British public is asked not to travel but they don't care. The whole bally lot are civilians on the spree. At Fleetwood thousands have been sleeping on pavements, waiting as long as two days to get to the Isle of Man. Stella Lucas had to stand twelve hours through the night to Glasgow, squashed in the luggage van. Another girl trying to return from Manchester off a job failed even to get on any morning trains. The amount of elderly women and mothers and babies traipsing about the country would amaze you.

I dread being sent out.

1 August 1943   HMS *Mercury I*, Haslemere, Surrey

I've had a frightful time in the last day or two. It's been unbearably hot. On Thursday night I set forth for London, sweltering in my shirt sleeves, and spent a warm clammy night at Ashley House.

At 6.30 am I arose, had breakfast and set out for Southend. Bear in mind, dearest, it's Bank Holiday weekend and the whole of

England and his wife are travelling. I got the only seat I could – in the middle of a third class compartment with no corridor. There were seven mothers with seven children, aged four to six, a woman with a golden retriever and a man with an overpowering cigar. I couldn't hear myself think. The children climbed all over the carriage with buckets and spades and the dog howled. Then two of the mothers began a vulgar brawl. One accused the other of taking up too much room, the other said that she'd paid for her ticket and was going to have as much bloody room as she bloody well liked.

It was very hot at Southend. In the burning sun I walked to my destination – and set off again an hour and a half later. The crowds at Liverpool Street were such that I had great difficulty getting my large gear across to Euston. Then I had the journey to Manchester, in a Pullman carriage with not one window that would open. The sun blazed in through the glass and I simply didn't know what to do with myself. The crowd in the train made the heat worse. Whew! I just sat and perspired, too overcome even to read.

At last we reached Manchester and I got rid of my gear, then away to the YMCA for the night. The woman there, who makes pets of all the couriers, put me in a room for four and said she would try to leave me on my own. I put on a nightie and lay down.

I had just fallen asleep when in came an enormous fat Waaf who proceeded to clump about the room for half an hour. No sooner had she at last got into bed than in came two more Waafs. They chattered and giggled and walked about and banged the door till I nearly screamed. About midnight they settled down, then, believe it or not, one coughed all night, one snored and the other ground her teeth.

I got about an hour's sleep.

8 August 1943   Tollgates Hotel, Battle, Sussex

Dearest Eric

Mummy and I came down here for my summer leave on Friday. A taxi met us at the little station at Battle and we drove through the village, then on and on till, to my horror, we landed out here plonk in the middle of the country – at a country house converted into a hotel and not even licensed! My heart sank.

It sank still more when I went into the lounge. There was positively no one under fifty! Fat old women with pet dogs in their laps were gossiping and elderly men were asleep behind their papers. You can't even bathe at Bexhill or Hastings because the beaches are all barbed wired and closed. Even the big open-air baths at the latter are closed. And there's nothing going on there at all.

Do you know what I've done since I came, my love? I've talked to old Dr Mills in his bath chair and played a little draughts with him. I've tried to read in the lounge but the old women insist on gossiping to me.

Dearest, I could cry from sheer depression. It's cold. It's also blowy, with sharp gusts of rain at intervals. If it wasn't for Mummy, I'd pack up and go and spend the rest of my leave in London, at Ashley House. Anything would be better than this mausoleum.

An elderly retired colonel and his wife eat at the next table to us. He makes noises, nasty sucking noises as he feeds. She is deaf and he has to repeat everything he says to her.

Last night I turned the wireless on – lovely music from the Continent – and Miss Clark with the Pom asked me to turn it off as she had a headache.

I've got a whole week more of this.

10 August 1943   Tollgates Hotel, Battle, Sussex

Dearest

My life of hectic and devastating excitement continues.

On Sunday Mummy, who hasn't seen the sea for five years, and I thought we'd go and visit Bexhill. I'd been there in peacetime: it was a pleasant seaside resort with crowds of people, large hotels, lovely glass pavilion on the front and lots going on.

It's rather different now. The streets are silent and deserted. The front is dreadful. Hotels are either demolished, gutted or boarded up. The glass of the pavilion is there still – but lying on the ground in pieces. Coils of barbed wire keep one well away from the beach. The gardens on the front have run wild. So have private gardens. Grass grows between the paving stones. It was cold, bleak and blowing a gale and eerie to a degree. A city of the dead, the only sound the sea roaring on the shingle. It's a derelict town.

We were shivering with the cold and needed a cup of tea. We actually found a hotel, not on the front, which was open. We were the only people in the big luxurious lounge. The desolation was unbelievable.

We'd no idea what it would be like.

Yesterday Mummy and I wandered down to Battle's flea pit and saw Charles Boyer in *Appointment for Love*. It was good entertainment.

I can't tell you how awful this hotel is – the old women with their pet dogs, the gaunt spinsters, the fat Jewesses. I talk most with a young boy of fourteen who's spending his summer holidays here with his parents. We swop stories of our prep school days and discuss the difficulties and hardships of Caesar's Gallic War translations, Pythagoras and logarithms and tell each other how wicked we were.

We were going to Hastings today but it's pouring with rain.

17 August 1943   HMS *Mercury I*, Haslemere, Surrey

Do you know what the Yanks are saying now? They are saying that Englishwomen are the most immoral in the world. Nice, isn't it?

And I'm really beginning to think it's true.

Coming down in the train opposite me were an American army officer and an attractive, well-dressed girl of the upper classes. They were sitting hand in hand and talking about the hotel they'd been staying in. They didn't look in the least married. When she made a neat little joke about her husband being at sea and what the eye didn't see, I felt rather sick.

Marie Thornton met a young United States Army Air Corps officer in a train the other evening and he saw her to Ashley House where she was going to stay the night. As they said goodbye he asked, 'Don't you want to sleep with me?' After Marie's strong answer he said, 'I'm awfully sorry, only you see I've been over here a month now and you're the first girl I've met who hasn't wanted an affair.'

Our daily papers are plastered with advertisements on venereal disease because it's become a national menace. Women's magazines are full of articles exhorting girls to live cleanly. The number of illegitimate children being born is so great that Parliament is fighting about marriage by proxy.

There are more prostitutes in London now than ever before. How they're not called up I don't know. Even society girls are joining their ranks.

I set forth on Saturday evening *en route* for King's Cross. I had a corner seat booked for me on the 10.25 to Newcastle. At Durham I changed. There are two places I have seen a fair amount of from train windows and have a desire to visit – Bath and Durham. Both have tremendously strong atmospheres, due no doubt to their great ages, and lovely houses and winding streets. As for Durham cathedral, it's one of the finest sights in England. It stands there on its hill, looking down on the old town, backed by woods and trees and rolling hills. Its architecture is simply wonderful.

I arrived in Sunderland about 7.30 am and asked for the RTO. I was told that there wasn't one and that I must go to the military police. I came to a dreadful tenement house in a back street and went up to the first floor as directed. I knocked on the door. Silence. I knocked again. A voice inside called, 'Orl right. Arf a tick.'

The door was opened, dearest, by a soldier swinging a towel and naked except for an open battledress blouse. He took one look at me, yelled and slammed the door. He was obviously not expecting a Wren.

In a few minutes he reappeared, very pink and better clothed, and then could give me no more information than a fly on the wall.

I had difficulty getting breakfast. The canteen was closed, the Grand Hotel catered for residents only and there was a quarrel about me at the Manor Commercial Hotel. I could hear a conversation below stairs, which went like this: 'I tell you we *don't* do breakfasts.' 'But it's a young girl and she's been travelling all night.' 'Tell her to go elsewhere.' 'Where else *can* she go?'

At last I got breakfast. I then made my way to the factory, where I struggled to make the police understand that I'd come to collect gear for Glasgow. They kept saying, 'Glass to go where?'

After an unpleasant phone conversation with the manager I learnt that the gear wouldn't be ready for twenty-four hours. A whole day to be spent in Sunderland. A sweet old foreman with a daughter in the WAAF insisted on escorting me to the YWCA. I slept the rest of the morning and in the afternoon took a bus to the very pleasant sea front. The beach was inaccessible of course. I went for a bit of a walk and had tea at the Grand Hotel in solitary state in an empty lounge.

Next morning I pottered around and visited the post office in the hope of sending you an airgraph but there were no forms and no pens. By midday I was away and was in Glasgow by nine that evening. I had to wait for my transport outside the station in the half dark. I shall never do that again!

The commander of the RN establishment was marvellous. We sat and chatted for half an hour, me cuddling his dachshund, then he called a wretched little Wren out of bed and told her to give me a good meal and anything I wanted.

Then, at 23.00, ensued a party in the galley – the Wren and I and two enormous sailors with beards. We had bread, ham, soup, jam and cocoa by the stove. The commander looked in twice to see how we were. I know he'd have loved to join us!

I slept at a comfortable service club in Glasgow and spent the next morning looking round. I explored Sauchiehall Street, Union Street, St Vincent Street, Bath Street – all famous and exactly like each other. It is a fine city, I must say.

27 August 1943   Perth

It's 22.45 and I'm sitting by myself in a reserved compartment in Perth station. The door and window say 'Reserved for Courier'. Hah! I can't help rather enjoying travelling in state while ferocious petty officers who would otherwise treat me like dirt are travelling third.

There are stars tonight, Eric, lovely stars. Our affair was wound about with stars and moonlight and always sunshine. There were no murky storms for us, were there, no petty jealousies and ugly scenes. It was too perfect to go on. I always knew something would happen, though your going away, thank God, hasn't stopped it. I think it's vastly improved it.

The journey up here has been pleasant. I was the only woman travelling first class so have had much kindness. We were six: a dear old skipper RNR of fisherman origin, now a sub-lieutenant; two warrant officers, both middle-aged; a sub-lieutenant; and a REME lieutenant. They took me along at teatime to the canteen truck on the end of the train, then when we got to Perth we all went and had dinner at the hotel. I was guest of the old skipper.

There's a two-hour wait here. This is the famous Jellicoe train for services only. It runs every day from Euston to Thurso for the Orkneys and north Scotland. Here at Perth it divides: the navy stays put and the RAF and army go into another train. An irate Waaf has just been fished out of the next compartment where she had a corner seat and sent packing to the other train. As I'm the only woman left now I'd have a compartment to myself if I were a courier or not.

When we pull out I shall roll up my mack as a pillow, curl myself up in my rug, take a couple of aspirin and try and sleep. Always in these dark hours in trains, lying sleepless, or in my bunk before I fall asleep or (rare thing) if I awaken early, my brain revolves round you, us, past and future. I have your last letters with me. I shall reread them again now, then prepare for 'bed'.

You can have the other side of the compartment if you like.

31 August 1943　　　The Dykeries, Compton, Guildford, Surrey

Dearest

I hardly know whether I'm coming or going. Have you had my serial letter written during the main part of my trip to the Isles? I expect you have so I'll continue from where I left off.

The next day was Sunday and I really feel I achieved something. Reasons – I did:

a. A sea trip
b. A plane flight
c. A train journey (over the Forth Bridge)
d. A lorry ride
e. A drive in an RN car
f. A train ride
g. And had dinner in Edinburgh with a little man in a bowler hat with walrus moustaches who was interested in boilers.

All this between 10.00 and 21.00! Don't you call that adventure?

Despite the fact that the weather conditions weren't awfully good I enjoyed the trip across the Flow. I'm well known now and am even greeted by the crew. 'Cor, you up 'ere again? 'Ow yer gettin' on?' The signaller thinks I'm 'ever ser sweet' and wants me to let him know when I'm next there. Poor signalman ...

The plane flight was awful. I've flown in high gales, snowstorms and other pleasures but this was worse than anything. The sky was black. We were tossed about like a cork. I wanted to die, dearest. I was as sick as a dog.

Suddenly there was the most awful noise. The plane shuddered and shook. We all looked at each other. Then there was less noise than there'd been before. Simultaneously with some gulls being caught up in the rigging one of the engines had gone wrong.

I was promptly sicker than ever.

When at last we landed we were driven to Inverkeithing. During the hour's wait for the train I sat in the canteen drinking tea with a fellow passenger, one of the Admiralty couriers, a retired naval officer. It was funny to talk shop with someone other than a Wren courier. We found our problems much the same, the main one being that the people that send us out on these trips have not the faintest idea of what the job is like. It was amusing to discover that the places we dislike the Admiralty couriers also dislike.

I spent a rather uncomfortable night in Edinburgh and came down yesterday on the day train.

I had a terrible time at the place in Orkney where I go to report. It's very isolated indeed so the advent of one of the very few couriers with any attraction at all is a major event. Work stops for the afternoon. I'm great pals with them all now (nothing to fear, dearest!).

This time they got me into a corner and systematically tried to discover if I was in love with anybody. I've never been so embarrassed. Paul, who's a great big middle-aged leading seaman, was a wealthy and aristocratic stockbroker in civil life. He's a bachelor and, I should think, an old *roué*. In his Mayfair drawl he said, 'You know, dear little Bolster, it's a brave man who takes you on, as you'll be a hell of a little pickle.' (Thought I'd better warn you!)

Lieutenant Parry, who's just got married, said I'd need beating once a week and Petty Officer Bottoms said that if he wasn't married himself he'd have a try at me, to see if I was tameable. Then we all went and had tea.

The sailor who was sent to escort me to the drifter said that he and his pals were anxious to see who was the cause of all work ceasing in the offices for the afternoon. I'd noticed him peeping through the windows previously.

8 September 1943   HMS *Mercury I*, Haslemere, Surrey

Isn't it wonderful about Italy?[1] It's really terrific – perhaps you'll be able to get home sooner now. It's the RAF's bombing that's done it mostly, I'm sure. You must be feeling good about it. I heard it when it was first announced, most dramatically, on the six o'clock news. We were told to stand by for the best news of the war.

Everyone felt like celebrating, only what can one do in a country dump like this? So, badly wanting a party of some sort, these poor Wrens had to work it off by going for walks in the fields or playing darts in the canteen. I went to bed early as I was done in. Lots of these girls have brothers or husbands or boyfriends as prisoners in Italy and they're feeling a hundred per cent.

I feel I've had a part in it as I've taken gear for lots of the ships concerned and for one very famous one, the day before she sailed.

9 September 1943   HMS *Mercury I*, Haslemere, Surrey

You never heard anything like the planes these days. Day and night enormous numbers of them simply roar overhead. At night it's positively deafening for hours on end. It's seldom that the sky is free from even a distant drone.

It's a comforting and satisfying thing to know that Plymouth and other ghastly tragedies have been avenged. But I hate all this bombing, whoever does it.

12 September 1943   Sick Bay, HMS *Mercury I*, Haslemere, Surrey

Dearest Eric

Come and look. The moon has just risen, full and early. The garden and the view are bathed in blue twilight. Soon there'll be stars. It's very lovely. This house on a hill is a wonderful refuge, a contrast to all the horrible big cities with their noise and dirt and smoke. I'm glad to do nothing for a day or two. I'm not ill or

---

[1] An armistice had been signed between Italy and the Allies on 3 September but was not made public until five days later. Italy's surrender proved something of a damp squib. The Germans immediately disarmed the Italian troops and seized control of the country.

anything, just a bit overworked and in need of a little reorganisation of digestion.

I'm on a diet of biscuits and Bovril, Epsom salts, tea and thin bread and margarine. Net result, I'm craving for food. What I could do to eggs and bacon!

15 September 1943   Sick Bay, HMS *Mercury I*, Haslemere, Surrey

Dearest Eric

There's an 'orrible 'orrible lack of mail. I haven't had anything all this week in Sick Bay, nor for five days before that, apart from your sea mail letter with photos. My output has been good just recently so hope you are getting mine. I guess it's this Italy business. What a mix up it's all been. I don't know why but I'm far more nervous about the battles around Salerno than I ever was about any of the North African campaigns. It's all most unsettling don't you find? I hate being in Sick Bay and at a time like this – I'd much rather be actively out and doing. I feel I ought to be rushing things up to Scapa or Greenock or Rosyth.

Life is deliciously quiet up here. I have a new title – 'GSA' – and I'm quite proud. It means 'Galley Stooge's Assistant'. I peel potatoes like a dream, take the seeds out of marrows like an expert, provide thousands of breadcrumbs for devious uses, make marvellous toast, gallons of tea. In fact, I earn my title.

18 September 1943   Sick Bay, HMS *Mercury I*, Haslemere, Surrey

Actually, Eric, it's selfish of me to keep on persuading you to come home. From my point of view there's *nothing* I want more – but from yours ... Well, quite honestly, you'd find life here a vastly different cup of tea. England's very much a country at war.

You will miss your continual swimming, afternoons of tennis, your parties and all your other recreations, which, to someone in England, sound like a peacetime existence.

You will come back to drabness, to rain and fog and cold, to rationing, to dreadful travel difficulties, high prices, probably harder work – an England where entertainment, except for drill hall hops, is very hard to find.

True, London carries on, but is so crowded with Yanks and

people that if you don't book a table in a restaurant a whole day or days before you won't even be allowed in. At lesser places you must stand in endless queues.

Shows are hard to get into too. Private entertaining practically everywhere has quite died out. Clothes are rationed as you know and evening dress worn very rarely.

So my advice to you, my love, is to continue your spree parties because you won't get them here!

24 September 1943   The Dykeries, Compton, Guildford, Surrey

Dearest

Things are moving! I came home this morning for the weekend and at teatime the phone went. It was the regulating petty officer informing me that my draft is through and that I report to some place in Portsmouth the day after tomorrow.

So it's come at last. Having waited five months I've very glad. I have a few regrets but very few. I shall never see Scapa Flow again or stand on Scrabster cliff looking across at the Orkney Isles, nor walk on Plymouth Hoe, nor gaze at Prince's Street, nor eat dried egg buns in Glasgow canteen, nor board a ship in the dead of night with secret things, nor feel really 'important' again.

But there'll be no more ghastly night trains, the terrible sleeplessness and dragging exhaustion, no more grubbing in dirty canteens, no more trailing round sordid factories, no more Manchester – I've broken the record for going there – no more creeping around Liverpool docks, no more noisy, dirty, jolting journeys and coughing crowds in airless compartments or waiting about in freezing cold stations in the middle of the night with eyes red and sore, no more frantic fights for porters, no more grim difficulties with enormous and heavy gear.

I shall have a bed every single night, Eric.

That is luxury – real luxury. I shall get clean and regular food. I shall see the back of those horrible old cats who always resented my youth and vivacity.

I hope I'll have a better bunk mate than the one I've got now. She's just like Popeye's Olive Oyl. She sits up in bed and screams in the night. Last night I swung my pillow over and hit her till she awoke – quite amiably!

26 September 1943   HMS *Mercury I*, Haslemere, Surrey

Dearest

The quarters are deserted. There's one cook in the galley and one courier getting ready to go out on a job. Everyone else has gone to divisions, inspection by the superintendent and church parade.

And me? Well, these are my last few minutes here. My case is packed and down at the station. My bunk is unmade, the blankets neatly covered by my quilt, and on my chair are gas mask, greatcoat and little attaché case.

And so life moves on. Here endeth another chapter, one of the most hectic, exciting and exhausting I shall ever have. I feel I've achieved something, having been a courier for eleven months and living at that speed.

There've been terrific goodbyes. The writers, stewards, cooks, special duties officers and all the new couriers have given me a grand send-off.

As for the old couriers, they're pleased to see me go but not nearly as pleased as I am to see the back of *them*!

Part Three

PART THREE

Wren Stoker   27 September 1943 – 25 June 1944

27 September 1943   HMS *Victory III*, Southsea

Dearest

I've really got what I want! I can ask no more of the service than this. I'm in lovely quarters in my favourite port with the sweetest girls you can imagine. I came down yesterday morning and reported to the drafting depot. The first thing that happened was a bottle (row) from the duty Wren in the hall for coming in by the front door instead of the ratings' entrance. I told her I couldn't know by instinct what I was expected to do.

In the afternoon I came round here to Summerlands. It's very pleasant as regards conditions and the food's terrific. There are seven of us on this course – only twenty-five have ever done it. We are ERA Wrens – Engine Room Artificers. Doesn't it sound gorgeous? The course lasts a month. It's the very same as the men's, the *leading* stokers.

We run around looking too terribly boats' crews with glamorous white lanyards draped round our necks and over our fronts. We have classroom instruction for two weeks. Our instructor is delightful, a dignified bald-headed little chief petty officer with rows of medals.

It's a very concentrated course indeed. Today we wrestled with the intricacies of four-stroke and two-stroke engines, pistons, valves, cylinders, camshafts, cranks, water pumping and all sorts of other things which, dearest, I didn't really understand a word about. After two weeks in class we have a week in the shops and a week on boats and are then drafted to establishments.

The dockyard is a wonderful place – colourful, ever-moving, a hundred per cent naval of course. One day I shall go over the *Victory* and see where Nelson died.

Dearest

I'm as happy as a sandboy here. I still don't understand magnetos but I'm becoming clear on the pumping system of diesel engines and I can just see how a four-stroke petrol engine works (suction, compression, power and exhaust), even if I'm a little vague on the twin-stroke. I seem to have learnt so much this week. On Wednesday we'll put on dungarees and go down into the shops. I feel that it'll be rather hard to apply the theory.

I know I'll be hopeless if anything goes wrong in my boat. I shall run and scream for a sailor.

I went to the barracks this morning to be kitted up for boats' crews. My dearest, I've so much gear I don't know what to do with it:

Two pairs bell bottoms
Two square-necked white sailor shirts
Two pairs woolly socks
Three pairs woolly stockings for under trousers
One lanyard
One seaman's jersey
Three pairs woolly bloomers (shall *never* wear them!)
Two dungarees
Two scarves
One seaman's knife
One pair boating shoes

All this as well as two suits, one greatcoat, mack, numerous shirts, collars, tie, nighties, stockings, shoes, dressing gown and ordinary underwear. Also a rug.

You can imagine what it'll be like going on draft, can't you?

Portsmouth's been dreadfully bombed and blitzed but there are a few places left for the services. The only hotel of any size still functioning is the Queen's.

There are little eating places that we go to and have sausage and chips. There's one called Moonrakers where I'll take you one day.

The sea front at Southsea is lovely. Unfortunately it's just too late in the year to bathe. Margaret and I went and sat on the beach the other night to watch the sunset but sailors started throwing stones at us so we had to move.

5 October 1943   Portsmouth Dockyard

Dearest Eric

Do you know what? We're *made* for each other!

I'm quite an engineer and, would you believe, I find pumps most interesting. I dote on the little fuel pump with anti-dribble valve on the diesel compression engine. It's awfully ingenious, isn't it? Are those the sort of pumps you used to design, dearest? I still find magnetos rather puzzling, though I can just understand coil ignition and I'm all there on carburation. Today is our last day in the classroom. I'm quite sorry, actually, as I enjoy the theory and I think I may find the practical hard.

I shall hate getting dirty nails and I don't fancy myself much in dungarees. We've spent the morning having a film show – demonstrating diesels. Pictures of bathing belles and pin-up girls appeared every so often to keep the sailors awake. It's now the lunch hour.

We bring two sandwiches each, then trip down to the galley with billy cans. Sailors give us soup out of an enormous boiler affair.

Half-way through the morning we have a stand-easy, ten minutes during which we jam on our sailor hats and run like mad for a low dive where we gulp down two-thirds of a glass of coffee, then rush back again.

I just couldn't be with nicer girls. We all get on so well and we have great fun. Margaret Boggis is just down from Oxford, having got a second in Greats. She's little and dark and podgy and sweet and not a bit 'learned'. Rozelle Pierrepont is the daughter of Countess Manvers. She's fair and slight and one hundred per cent well bred. She's only eighteen and we all love her. Tim Edridge is wild, has red hair and exuberance. She's a great friend of Laurence Olivier and Vivien Leigh. Patsy Thomas is horses mad. Her mother is a famous racer. Patsy has few other interests but riding. Jean Campbell is one of the nicest-natured girls you could find. She's man crazy – a typist from Sunderland. Then there is Anne Norris, who is small and fair and the daughter of a well-known business man.

Am writing now in class, hoping Chief won't see. He's explaining diesels to Tim. She can't understand anything and is terrified of failing. I'll probably keep her company. Oh Lor, I'll get caught any minute.

I'd much rather learn engineering from you, dearest!

111

9 October 1943   HMS *Victory III*, Southsea

I have had an amusing week as regards work. Attired in amazing dungarees we've been in the engine rooms. All by myself I pulled a Ford V20 engine to bits, then built it up – and it went. I nearly died of surprise.

Yesterday I was sitting perched up learning to work the ahead and astern gear when an admiral, a general and attendants came along on a tour of inspection. Of course they had to come and ask me what I was doing – and I felt a complete mug in my dungarees.

On Monday we start going in boats. I've an insatiable desire to go in an MTB.

11 October 1943   HMS *Victory III*, Southsea

I must tell you, I've had such an adventure.

In my last letter I described how a friend of mine on this course, Rozelle Pierrepont, turned out to be the daughter of Countess and Earl Manvers. Also that she invited Margaret Boggis and me to dinner at the Queen's last night to meet her people.

Well, Margaret and I were up in the cabin getting ready, brushing up our tiddley suits, cleaning our shoes and trembling at the idea of meeting the earl and countess when Rozelle burst in with a ghastly piece of news.

Her father had asked the superintendent of the Wrens to dinner also!

Do you know what that meant, Eric? It was exactly the same as two aircraftman IIs being asked to meet an air vice-marshal.

I was nearly sick from fright. My tie wouldn't go right, I lost my stud, my hair wouldn't behave.

It was bad enough to be meeting the higher aristocracy, let alone the superintendent. We felt our careers were at stake.

At last, nearly mental from apprehension, we walked into the Queen's. We ploughed through all the gold braid till we found Lord Manvers.

He turned out to be sweet – great sense of humour and kind. I relaxed slightly. The countess then made her entrance. She was good-looking and reasonably amiable but spoke so softly I couldn't hear half of what she said and she was also heavy going.

Then in swept the superintendent followed by the eyes of all naval personnel, especially Wren officers. Her grey hair was drawn tightly under her tricorne. The strain was shocking.

On the way to the dining room Margaret's shoes squeaked dreadfully and that made us want to giggle. Everyone looked up when we came in and there must have been much wondering who the Wrens with milord, milady and the superintendent were.

The meal could scarcely have been more formal. The food was good but I could hardly enjoy it. I was badly placed, being between Lady Manvers and Margaret. It was interesting that I'd been a courier. So I'd been six times to Scapa Flow. A pity I'd never managed Ireland. But not much else was said.

It was overwhelmingly hot. I thought I'd expire if I didn't take my jacket off.

With burgundy the atmosphere eased. After four glasses old super became quite jovial. Lord Manvers began to tell stories and Lady Manvers became a little easier to talk to. Coffee in the lounge was all right – I got Lord Manvers telling me his experiences in the last war.

We had to be in by ten and we walked slowly back beneath the stars, exhausted, glad of the experience but mighty glad it was over.

None of the Wrens would believe who we'd dined with. It sounded too impossible.

12 October 1943   HMS *Victory III*, Southsea

Dearest

I've had a wonderful day. I've spent it driving round Portsmouth harbour in a speedboat, whizzing across the sunlit sea with the bows out of the water and a long wash of foam behind. There's nothing to it – clutch, rudder, wheel and throttle. Easy! We had a crew of three sailors, coxswain (instructor), stoker and deckhand. I took them to Gosport and nearly to Spithead. The exhilaration was terrific.

This morning we went over the harbour to get the rum ration for our establishments but I wasn't allowed even a smell!

15 October 1943   HMS *Victory III*, Southsea

I must tell you what happened last Saturday night. Tim Edridge, who's quite mad (she's got red hair and freckles) and I decided we'd go dancing at a low dive for a shilling. Just for adventure – the sort of thing one can do in uniform and not out of it. So we put on our tiddley suits and, feeling a little nervous, off we went. The actual hall wasn't bad, it was just the company – toughs, sailors, soldiers, negroes, half-castes, barmaids and so on.

We stood there for a few minutes, then Tim espied a sailor she knew. As soon as she'd gone I was suddenly dragged on to the floor by the most awful Pole you ever saw. He had a bright blue suit, ginger hair, enormous curling ginger mustachios and leering slit eyes. He hugged me round the floor for three consecutive dances, behaving in a dreadful fashion. Just when I was getting desperate I managed to slip away and ran panting to Tim in the bar.

I was then picked up by a little sailor with black curly hair, who came from Manchester. He was 'decent' but very dull. When he said, 'Eee, ah moost see thee again. Can I take thee t' cinema Wednesday?' I felt the time had come to make a move to the ladies' room.

When I came out I was landed with a Royal Marine who had a cold and had lost his voice. Conversation consisted of much hissing and gasping with intermittent croaking on his part and rather bewildered answers from me.

About 10.30 they played 'God Save the King'. I was looking for Tim when the dreadful Pole appeared and announced that he was seeing me home!

I informed him that he was not. I couldn't find Tim outside in the dark and I was quite scared. Then the Pole appeared again. I took to my heels and ran. To my horror he followed, calling out. I heard him coming nearer and nearer. I snatched off my sailor cap, undid my jacket and sprinted for all I was worth.

How far I was followed I do not know. My tale was a great source of amusement to the others, all vastly intrigued by my breathless rush into the cabin.

18 October 1943   HMS *Victory III*, Southsea

We went to sea this afternoon, three of us, as a special and unofficial concession. We went in a motor launch – very fast – and my God it was rough. Rozelle quickly succumbed but I didn't feel a twinge. We were soaked in no time. We rolled and pitched and I was thrown from side to side, my face stiff from salt spray. It was somewhat overcoming but terribly exciting.

We felt rather pleased to have done it when we got in wet and laughing as just after we'd gone orders had been given that no small craft were to leave harbour because of the roughness!

19 October 1943   HMS *Victory III*, Southsea

What is the difference between coil ignition and the magneto and *how* do you explain it? And please, I don't yet understand the advance and retard of ignition. Whatever shall I do? The blessed exam's the day after tomorrow.

I swot and swot and things don't go in and I'm getting the panics. It's a three-hour paper and I've *got* to pass.

The other day I . . . er . . . I . . . er . . . rammed a yacht! I did, really. A coxswain and deckhand took us out in a skimmer, three of us. It was heaven. We sped like the wind in and out and round about over the sunlit waters and took turns in learning to drive. I was doing fine, then coxswain told me to encircle a large and stationary yacht. And – well I just rammed it, that's all.

There were loud cries from the stern sheets, one or two rude exclamations from the deckhand but kindness from coxswain.

I won't do it again.

25 October 1943   HMS *Victory III*, Southsea

I had a super weekend in London. On Saturday evening I went to the Renaissance Club. It was amusing. Very *demi-monde* – thick smoky atmosphere, a few people hugging each other round a tiny square of dance floor, haggard women plastered with make-up, debauched-looking men with rings under their eyes, everyone calling everyone else 'darling', all more or less drunk and propping each other up round the bar. Their conversation was utterly inane. I drank more than was good for me and received a lot of absurd and insincere compliments.

Towards the end of the evening my head suddenly cleared and I felt completely detached from the drinking, smoking, hard-boiled crowd. I thought of the *Georgia Fane* and her bows rising out of the water, the speed of her, the clear bright air and the wind and the spray, the harbour and the gulls, the sailors calling to each other. And I felt sorry for all those people because they don't know the things I know. And I thought too of Hurdlefoot and Radwell and the well at Stevington and I wondered if any of them were ever happy like that. They didn't look it.

I'd so much rather be a sailor than a night club queen!

Dearest Eric

Have you had my airgraph telling you I was second in my engineering exam? Well, it's a mistake. They made a gaffe in the marking and it transpired that I'm top with 89 per cent. Isn't it amusing?

I've been congratulated by the captain, who told me to apply to him if I ever got into difficulties (ie in the boats!).

I've actually beaten Margaret, who is a BA, and also another girl who's done this work before and spent the whole of the course knowing everything. If I ever asked Chief a question she always chipped in with the answer.

And so it's all over and we left Flathouse for good this morning. I was dreadfully sad about it. We made so many friends and loved the work. We were the only Wrens there, so were well looked after. We ran down to the jetty before we left and said goodbye to the little boats we went out in and their sailor crews. As we passed through the gates the sailors all cried, 'Cheerio, stokies, best of luck!' and I could easily have wept.

3 November 1943   HMS *Victory III*, Southsea

Our drafts were expected on Tuesday but they never happened, so we go on charring. I don't mind. I'm used now to organising the housework. 'Margaret, will you please do the main deck and polish the floor. Anne, will you do cabin "Plymouth" and for the love of Mike don't forget behind the chests of drawers. And I'll sweep and scrub the back stairs.' We all giggle about it and if it's a bit tedious, well it's only for another day or two (we hope).

The stoker badges on our sleeves cause quite a furore wherever we go – just a blue propellor but it's almost unknown on Wrens. Coming out of church on Sunday about four of us were half way down the aisle when a pewful of sailors espied us and there was nearly a riot. 'Cor, look, stokers!' 'Ere, watcher doing in them badges?' 'Cooee, stokies!' 'Whoopee!' 'Wot's on the end of yer lanyards?' 'Can I 'elp rev up yer engine?'

We hurried on quickly, followed by many a navy blue eye. It's quite fun to be a novelty.

9 November 1943   HMS *Victory III*, Southsea

Dearest

It's such lovely weather! Cold and clear and blue sky and autumn golds and reds and that certain tang in the air that makes you want to run and laugh just because you're young and life seems to be going so incredibly smoothly for once.

On Sunday Rozelle and I thought we'd go and explore Hayling Island in the afternoon. We set forth wearing our greatcoats for the first time this season as it was nippy.

We took a train to Havant, got out and took a bus to Hayling Island. It was a long and not uninteresting ride. We alighted on the south coast and found beautiful sands, with a blue sea far out. We walked along the beach for a while, then, feeling rather cold, we began to look for somewhere to have tea. Little sign of civilisation – a few mouldy buildings in a long straggling line. Being Sunday, everywhere was closed. Then we came across a dive called The Grotto. It said 'Snack Bar Café'. We tried the door – and to our horror a crowd of the most *awful*-looking men appeared at the windows, calling out to us to come in. Needless to say, we disappeared. At last we got a cup of cold tea at a lorry drivers' den. By then it was about 5 – so we went and queued for a bus. After half an hour of stamping in the cold we had the pleasure of seeing the last two buses sail past, crowded to the doors. Not a chance of hitch-hiking to Havant, as there was no traffic.

Rozzy then had the bright idea of going to some naval place to ask if they'd any transport bound for the mainland. We made our way there and a conceited ass of a sub-lieutenant informed us that there was no transport and the only thing we could do was walk miles to the ferry across the harbour to see if we could catch the last one.

It was late twilight. We set off along the road, soon leaving any signs of civilisation behind us. To right, left and ahead were miles of waste, mud flats, scrub and wild skies. Not a hill to be seen – just flatness. We walked very hard for an hour and a half. It was incredibly eerie. A shrouded moon got up behind us. The most harmless bird seemed like something sinister. We could see no sign

of any ferry. I kept thinking of Canadian murders of girls on
Thursley Common and such places.

At last a few shapes appeared in the dimness. Just a few derelict
buildings, mostly half fallen down. Not a breath of life, not a sound.
We ran down a sort of pier place at the end of which were moored
a couple of old boats. I called out, 'Ahoy there. Anyone about?'

Silence. Rozelle and I looked at each other, both with the same
vision of that ghastly walk back.

I called again. By a miracle a sailor appeared out of a boat. I
nearly fell on his neck.

He told us the last ferry had gone an hour before! Anti-climax.

He called a pal and we explained the situation. Because we were
fellow sailors they volunteered to take us over unofficially and risk
a bottle. Quietly we slipped away into the night. The moonlight
was wonderful. There was a great path of silver across the water.
Of course we had to be found out! Along came a launch and a lot
of shouting went on while Rozzy and I kept under cover but it
seemed all right in a moment or two.

We landed at a desolate place on the mainland. None of us knew
where. We bid a grateful farewell to our rescuers and set forth. We
walked for three hours – more wild wastes, flats, marshes – and still

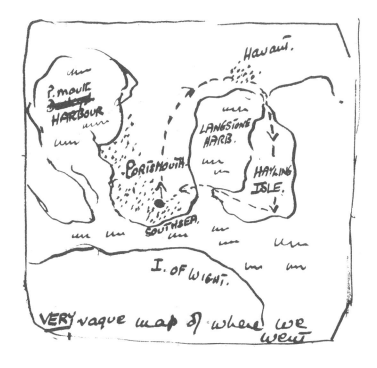

that incredible eeriness. It was certainly romantic though a bit chilly. The stars were coldly bright.

At last we came across a chief petty officer on a cycle who told us that the main Eastney road wasn't far off. Eventually we picked up a bus and got back to Southsea, where we had another walk to quarters and arrived well adrift, with everyone dying to know what had happened.

Did I sleep well after it all or did I!

15 November 1943   HMS *Shrapnel*, Southampton

Dearest

I have had the most *fantastic* experience, which I want to tell you all about.

I went for the weekend to Thoresby Park, somewhere in England, as the guest of Earl and Countess Manvers. I was somewhat nervous about it, dearest, knowing it would be a huge house, formal and so on, but I was naturally pretty excited.

Rozelle and I got away from Portsmouth about 2.30 and had a crowded but not too awful journey. As we drew into a station, Rozzy said, 'This is X – ours is the next.' Whereupon I went along to wash and had got as far as standing with one hand holding a loofah and the other filling the basin when outside there were cries of 'Maureen, Maureen, quick, we're here after all.' I fell out of the train with loofah and sponge bag in one hand, hat on the back of my head, gas mask round my waist, gloves between my teeth and case in the other hand.

While I was organising myself we heard to our amazement a band playing on the platform. It was a lovely effect to arrive by starlight and moonlight and have a military band to welcome us. Spellbound we listened for a while, then went out to the chauffeur-driven car that awaited us.

We had a long cross-country drive. At last we swept through great gates and were in the park. Miles and miles of drive – visions of great sweeps of pasture, woods, herds of deer, lakes and so forth.

Then, turning a corner, there was Thoresby. Dearest, from that moment I entered a dream because I could not believe that all I saw was true. I've seen great buildings but this had a vast magnificence that nothing else could compare with. And standing there in the moonlight the beauty and romantic aspect of it was indescribable.

We alighted from the car beneath a massive porch. Immediately servants were there to open doors and cope with luggage. My first impression of the interior was of enormous space and height – great staircases, stone pillars, portraits, suits of armour, flowers – then we came into the great hall. That nearly finished me off. I stood completely tongue-tied. It reached to roof level, several storeys high, of such a height that by night the ceiling was scarcely visible. Its width and length I can only leave to your imagination. Also the swords, large paintings on the walls, the huge fireplace with log fire burning, the galleries and alcoves, the main staircase at the far end, the pillars . . .

Across the shining polished floor glided Lady Manvers in evening dress. She received us graciously and called servants to see us to our rooms. Mine was big, with double bed, many mirrors and exquisite hangings and furniture.

When Rozelle and I descended, we went in to the dining room for a late dinner together, the houschold having long finished. The beautiful table was laden with heavy and wonderful silver, lovely flowers and glass. We had soup, a meat dish, hock, a cream trifle done in gin, cheese straws and port. Just an *ordinary* dinner.

It was extraordinary to see Rozzy sitting there attended by butlers and servants – 'Yes, Milady. No, Milady' – Rozzy who helps us wash up greasy dishes, dances at the pier for a shilling and scrubs the back stairs.

The countess came in to discuss the Guards ball for the following evening. His Highness Prince Bernhard of the Netherlands was coming, Her Grace the Duchess of Portland and other distinguished people. My feeling of daze increased.

After dinner I was led to the vast ancestral library to meet the company – Lady Ruth Balfour and Colonel Balfour[1] and various extremely stiff-looking Guards officers who were standing rigidly around. They were in mess dress and I had the absurd idea that if you pushed them they'd fall over without changing position.

About 11.30 Rozzy extricated us on the excuse of a long journey and the ball on the morrow. By that time, dearest, I was nearly prostrate from fright. I didn't see how I was going to cope. Feeling like an ant, I crept into my imposing room and having finished my toilet sank into the double bed. My head was going round and

[1] Colonel (later Brigadier) William Sturgis Balfour, 1888–1955. Officer Commanding Scots Guards Regiment and Regimental District, 1934–1938 and 1939–1943.

round. I asked myself what on earth I thought I was doing in this nobleman's world of great aristocrats and wealth – I should have guessed it was miles above my element. What the hell would I do if confronted by royalty and how to cope with a duke? Supposing I were to do the wrong thing – address people incorrectly, spill something.

I was awoken in the morning by a maid who came to draw the curtains. Breakfast was very formal and dignified but I felt at my ease and actually enjoyed it.

About 10.30 a fleet of army cars drove up to take the house party across the park to attend a great regimental parade. The old colonel (Balfour – the one staying in the house) was retiring and he was having a farewell inspection. The sun shone, the wind blew, it was all very 'county' and you may see my picture in *The Tatler*! Everyone seemed to be titled and very pukka indeed.

Afterwards Rozelle and I chose to walk back via the lake, which is several miles long and superbly beautiful. Lunch was long and involved – marvellous food, of course – and afterwards Lord Manvers took Colonel and Lady Balfour, their daughter and me for a tour of the park in 'Lightning'. This was an amazing contraption, an electric car – no petrol needed. It does 14 mph and can only get up little hills but is wonderful when there's nothing else.

Soon after tea Rozelle and I retired to get ready for the ball. A log fire was blazing in my room and my dress, beautifully ironed, was laid out on my bed. I was, of course, hopelessly excited. At 7 o'clock Lady Manvers sent in a hairdresser who'd been imported and I felt so very grand.

At a quarter to eight we came down. I was told by various kindly people that I looked very well. My dress was as fine as any there – blue and gold, the whole thing shimmering in the light and falling in heavy and graceful folds. Around my neck and waist was some blue and gold jewellery given me by Peter Russell. The material for the gown was bought for me in Paris by Aunt Hess just before the war. I designed it and it's one of the loveliest things I've got.

Rozelle was in a full and simple frock of pale blue net. It suited her fragile appearance.

We were twelve to dinner. I sat between Lord Manvers and a snooty Guards captain. We had soup and sherry, lobster mayonnaise followed by pheasant with queer trimmings and champagne, then some elaborate and highly creamed sweet with more wine, then cheese straws, fruit and port.

After dinner, feeling remarkably well fed, I went upstairs with the other women and came down to the ball.

Dearest, I cannot attempt to describe to you the incredible glamour of the occasion. Can you imagine that vast ballroom filled with the flower of the English aristocracy, the decorations, the band of fifteen from London, the Guards in mess dress, the girls in ball frocks?

Great men and women made their entrances, medals abounded, huge rooms led to other enormous rooms and tables were laden with delicacies from London – I've never seen so much food in my life. Drink was unlimited – champagne, claret cup, whisky, cider cup and heaven knows what.

I had a marvellous time. I can't tell you who I danced with because for the most part I don't know – wonderful-looking six footers, aristocrats, aloof, lovely dancers and amazingly lacking in conversational ability. They all looked more or less the same and all said the same things. The girls were much alike too – highly bred, fresh-looking and with a similar manner and expression. People had come from all over the country for this, the first ball the Guards had given since the war began.

It made me feel what a very wonderful thing England is. All this beauty, fineness, grace and dignity is ours and no other country has it. And although most of our aristocracy is awful there are many who are great and you felt there that night that if a country could achieve such a civilisation as this it could never fail.

Half-way through four Yank officers and four WAACs arrived in uniform. They slouched round the room chewing gum, wearing rimless glasses and pouting their thick flabby lips. It was incredible how out of the picture they looked and how they clashed with the atmosphere.

Beautiful music was played – Strauss, Weber, even Brahms waltzes – not a hint of jitterbugging or congaing. I was in a complete haze when at a quarter to four I tumbled into bed.

Unfortunately Rozelle and I had been recalled by wire so instead of being able to recuperate we had to spend the day travelling, in a sort of coma, still overcome with glamour!

As an experience, Eric, it's one I'm terribly glad to have had. You see, I had no idea at all how those people lived, in fact had no conception of such a thing. In time of war it was all the more fantastic. I don't think I've yet got it quite in proportion.

I do know this, though, I'd rather live at another Dykeries and have a little room with pink fittings and eat in the kitchen and have a country garden with a Jersey herd grazing on the hill behind. I know too I'd rather have you and go to country pubs with you than all the stiff and aloof and doll-like Guards officers in Christendom.

18 November 1943   H M S *Shrapnel*, Southampton

You know by now that I'm in Southampton. I'm quartered in a great big luxury hotel taken over. The Wrens live on the top floor. They are nice rooms with hot and cold. Next week I'm moving into a wedding suite room with luxury bathroom off it. I'm sure the builders never foresaw our double decker bunks and serviceable chests of drawers.

We have 130 steps to climb and our mess is on the ground floor, four storeys below! Imagine me hurtling down to my breakfast. We're centrally heated, thank heavens.

About my place of work,[1] dearest, I can tell you nothing, much as I'd like to. All I can say is that I like it a lot, that it's *perishing* cold and that we're pioneers, being the first and only boats' crew. We are considered a great speciality and we might be somewhat spoilt.

As for *Anndora II*, she's the finest ship that sailed the seven seas. We're seven in crew. Our coxswain's Leading Seaman Clarke, who goes all pink when he speaks to us. He knows how to handle a boat though. I'm No. 2, being senior engineer (!?!), then there are the other stokers, Margaret and Rozelle, and lastly the three deckhands, Tim Edridge, who was with us at Portsmouth but failed the exam,

124   [1] H M S *Abatos*.

and a girl called Pamela Desoutter, who's rather attractive but we're not quite sure yet if we like her, and Benny, who's only eighteen and *very* worthy and 'Girl Guides' but is rather sweet.

We have a lovely wheelroom, with all sorts of gadgets, a big and comfy cabin, masses of cupboards, two washbasins, a lavatory, a nice deck and a dear little engine room with twin petrol engines.

We are very busy between trips, as odd naval officers are detailed off to teach us semaphore, wireless transmitting and receiving, morse, seamanship and knots. I love semaphore. I love doing it with flags while out on the water. I'm finding wireless a bit hard, though I did enjoy saying dirty rude things to Germany this morning. As for knots, I no sooner learn one sort than I try another and forget the first. Still, it's all intensely interesting. And it's such fun running about in bell bottoms, white plimsolls, navy jackets, white lanyards and our hats on the back of our heads. We do look smashing and arouse a lot of comment. We're the only boats' crew in the whole of that hotel and as our uniform is most distinctive we get much gawped at.

I had some trouble with an old lieutenant-commander RNR, who came aboard and fired questions about the engine at me, one after the other. The engine (starboard one) wouldn't start yesterday afternoon and I was sure it was the fuel system. He said it was the battery and sent someone to get a new one. I opened up the distributor, opened the circuit breaker points and there was a huge spark. It turned out to be carburation trouble.

Did I gloat!

22 November 1943   HMS *Shrapnel*, Southampton

The days have been filled with engine room consultations with stokers and mechanics, semaphore lessons and practice, knotting and splicing, cleaning engines, rushing full speed across the water, sitting in the boiler room (on a plank) in the establishment trying to get warm, making ship's cocoa and learning a little easy sculling and rowing.

Unhappily *Anndora*'s engines are not good. Today one rotor arm broke and a leak occurred in a petrol pipe. Yesterday we had bad sparking plug trouble, and not for want of maintenance either. She has too much rust and corrosion for my liking and her fuel system is unreliable.

Funny the affection one can get for an engine, isn't it? Mine is quite unreasoning as I much prefer a petrol engine with its attendant troubles to a diesel, which, between you and me, rather scares me.

We haven't been able to do as many trips as we should have done, owing to *Anndora*'s indisposition, but she'll be well soon, we hope.

I cleaned all her metal work with Bluebell and she looks smashing.

25 November 1943   HMS *Shrapnel*, Southampton

Coxswain is taking advantage of *Anndora*'s indisposition to go away for a week's leave. We all 'love' him. He's the nicest type of sailor in the Royal Navy, and that's saying a lot. He's engaged to a lorry driver in the WAAF and we do hope she's worthy of him.

He is little, red-faced, a leading seaman and, my God, there isn't much he doesn't know about seafaring. He's been on Russian convoys, been torpedoed and blown up and heaven knows what.

You will like my hair — there's not a hair grip in it! You knew it like this: —

it's now like this: —

it's thick & curly all over my head, & the only restraining influence is the way it's cut — & it's much more "glam" than before.

He calls us by our Christian names now. He forgets sometimes in front of officers: 'Maureen, er Stokes, will you . . .'

Today Coxswain produced a beautiful green woolly dog called Ploogle. We promptly made him our mascot.

26 November 1943   HMS *Shrapnel*, Southampton

This afternoon we had rowing instruction. Our Wren crew with sailor coxswain raced a sailors' crew with officer coxswain and – well, they won. Did my arms ache! I don't believe in taking rowing seriously. It's best for ambling about rivers in the summer. It was a beautiful afternoon and I must say it was most pleasant out there on the water.

I liked doing morse this morning. Do you understand it, dearest? Here is a vital message for you ——— And here's another ——— (Sorry, mix-up, I'll start again.) Here's both messages in one:

```
. .    . — . .    — — —    . . —    .    — . — —
— — —    . . — . —    . — —    . — — .    . .
. —    — —    . — . .    — — — —    — . —    — —   .
. .    — . .    — — . — .    . — . .    — — — . — . —
— . —    — — . — . — .    . — .    . — .
. — . .    — . . .    — . — .    — — . .   1
```

And how!

7 December 1943   HMS *Shrapnel*, Southampton

I steel myself not to think about your return in case something should go wrong and make me die of disappointment, yet my mind wanders.

This sort of thing happens during my seamanship studies: shg on a chart denotes shingle, r = rock, conical buoys must be left to starboard when sailing with the tide – how glorious to have a night out in London as soon as he comes back – cylindrical buoys mark fairways and a thing with a pole the entrance to a harbour – we

---

[1] I love you and I am longing for your return.

could dine at *L'Ecu de France* again and go and watch the Thames by night and the tugs going up and down – a can-shaped buoy must be left to port . . .

We're a bit fed up as *Anndora*'s still in dock. The captain's furious about it and would give anything to get her going. We feel that we don't earn the right to our lanyards at the moment.

Social life in Southampton doesn't show much sign of being any good. It's such a mix-up of a place – and not one where a girl could be out alone at night. Did I tell you that we got sick of some drunks screaming and shouting under our window the other night so we got a bucket of water and heaved it out?

Splash! Silence. Then a dreadful stream of oaths. We climbed back into our bunks, satisfied.

We keep a bucket full of water under our washstand every night now.

10 December 1943   The Dykeries, Compton, Guildford, Surrey

I did have an experience the other night. Pam Desoutter and I went to a dance at the American Red Cross. We were dragged in at the door by an individual with rimless glasses, black curly hair, thick lips and a sallow face. 'Come in, girls, enjoy yourselves. Do what you like. You're welcome.'

When we'd taken off our coats a nice little woman in Red Cross uniform got hold of us and said, 'Now, girls, I must warn you. Don't be upset if they don't dance with you at first but the boys are a bit bashful and need a little encouraging.'

Well, er, that wasn't our impression. We were immediately set upon by some more rimless glasses. What a room it was. Stars and stripes all over the walls, pictures of women in underclothes and lots of Yanks lounging about aimlessly chewing. They were hospitable, I must say that, and the food was incredible but their manners were so awful. They did nothing but criticise England the whole time. I was slowly getting more and more worked up.

At the end of the evening a Yank naval officer badly overstepped the mark about England and the English and a rather vulgar brawl took place.

I was simply bristling with patriotism. How dare those Yanks come here and run my country down!

I let forth hotly. The Yank naval officer got a bit uncomfortable, then tried to change the atmosphere – most unsubtly. 'Say, I'll see you home. Gee, I guess you'll be nice to hug!'

I coldly informed him he would not have the chance – and left him gaping on the floor.

Pam implored me to go home with her and a Yank soldier she didn't trust but couldn't shake off. He was furious at my presence so we were a funny trio.

14 December 1943   HMS *Shrapnel*, Southampton

What do you think I discovered when I got back here from leave, dearest? *Anndora II* was sunk and is lying on the ocean bed!

Margaret had discovered a bad leak and reported it at once to the officer, who promptly forgot. So *Anndora* sank gracefully during the night and she's not up yet.

The captain does *not* think it's funny.

20 December 1943   HMS *Shrapnel*, Southampton

We're running a big diesel launch at the moment, Eric. She's not as fast as *Anndora II* but she's got a much nicer engine room and is vastly more reliable. We've done some good trips in her. It's lovely being a stoker as when it gets awfully cold you can disappear quietly into the engine room and hug the exhaust pipe!

We've got nicknames at the base now. The majority of the sailors don't know our names, so refer to Benny as 'Lofty', Margaret as 'Darkie', Pam as 'Spam', Rozelle as 'Blondie' (as if her fragile fairness resembled in the slightest the garishness of peroxided blondness), Tim as 'Ginger' and I am known as 'Curly'. And sometimes as 'Curly Stokes'.

Dearest

I'm as snug as a bug in a rug in a fug in a tug! It's Christmas Eve. I'm well tucked up in my bunk and at the end of it hangs a large white seaboot sock. I've bagged to be first to be Father Christmas after lights out.

We've done a hard day's work today. Because the men were on leave we had to set to and clean out the dinghies in the freezing cold. We came back to a concert in the men's mess. It was fun – amateurish and all that but amusing – and everyone was in the mood to enjoy it.

One turn was most uncalled for. A perfectly frightful Wren did a very clumsy striptease by shadow behind a thin sheet and it caused a lot of comment from all sides. It was considered very out of place. Still, the rest of the show more than made up for it and we got a good laugh.

I wonder what will be in my sock in the morning.

Dearest

Oh Lor! My head, my ankles, my tum! I'm in bed. Downstairs a dance is in progress but really I've no strength for it.

I must say I've had one of the best Christmases I've ever known. After lights out on Christmas Eve we took it in turns to flounder about in the dark with a torch being Father Christmas. Much scuffling, dropping of parcels, giggling and fumbling. We'd taken charge of each other's parcels so that nothing should be looked at before Christmas Day.

It was lovely waking up yesterday morning. We all sat on our bunks undoing parcels as hard as we could. 'Oh, just look!' 'This *is* nice.' 'Just what I wanted.'

Mummy sent me a homemade cake, a few biscuits, a nice box of face powder and a smashing blue wallet. Margaret gave me two beautiful books of music – Chopin's 'Ballades' and 'Fifteen Waltzes'. Benny gave me a buttonhole and a pretty painted face cream jar. Rozelle gave me a little hairbrush and comb in a swagger box and Pam gave me something I've wanted for years – the book of Pont's drawings from *Punch*, the British Character series. I must show it to you when you come home. We'll sit by the fire and have a good laugh together over it.

Lord Manvers sent me a bottle opener with corkscrew, which he said no stoker should be without, and Lady Manvers sent me a book. Aunt Hess sent me some lovely necklaces and a blouse, and I had money from one or two aunts and people.

Our cabin is a mass of Christmas cards. It has amused us how many people have sent us ones with ships on this year.

We had real eggs for breakfast, then went to church in a little chapel in the Missions to Seamen where we sang carols lustily with the sailors.

Christmas lunch was wonderful. Turkey, plum pudding and apples – and the officers waiting on us. Huh – almost the best part of the meal that! Afterwards there was a scavenger hunt for those who wished. I'm afraid we made a bolt for the best armchairs in the recreation room.

At 5.30 there was high tea in the sailors' mess, the whole room one mass of sailors and Wrens. The sailors here, actually, are not proper ones. They don't wear square rig but ordinary suits or fore and aft rig and look just like civilians. They're mostly about seventeen and are electrical trainees, being in a low physical category. They are nearly all very weedy and incredibly spotty.

Later the party began. There were about 200 there. Some Yank soldiers had been invited and they lolled about chewing gum and looking the Wrens up and down. We asked coxswain and he came all spruce in his Number Ones, dreadfully shy, rubbing his chin and going all pink. He was a great success. Everyone loved him.

There were games and dancing and community singing and all sorts of jollifications. There was an egg and spoon race and the petty officer in charge asked for two seamen to compete with two stokers. The former were easily obtained but there didn't seem to be any of the latter present. Suddenly an unknown grabbed Rozelle and me, shoved us onto the floor and called out, 'Here are two stokers!' This caused a huge sensation. Everyone barracked and shouted, 'Come on stokes! Run, go it, go it, stokes!'

All this went on till 2.30. Halfway through, the Wren and naval officers descended from the wardroom, all quite boozy. They didn't fit in with the atmosphere at all and everyone was very glad when they went. One Wren officer was so far gone that the first officer ordered her removal.

Our lights went out at about three this morning.

5 January 1944   The Dykeries, Compton, Guildford, Surrey

I loved your letter cards of 20 and 21 December, which came today. Hum ... yes, I think my idea of you is pretty close to your list of admissions. I think I'll have a go at myself!

a. Five feet six inches, weight about 9 stone, well proportioned.
b. Hair brown and curly, eyes brown, flecked gold, green and red.
c. Teeth fair, not as good as they look, eyesight A1, hears more than necessary on occasions.
d. Complexion fresh. No spots, moles, scars or hairs.
e. Irish and hot-blooded, energetic, impulsive and impetuous. Needs some control and a strong will.
f. Passionately loves beauty and must have it – could not live in Industrial North. Loves great music (not Bach, not romantic enough, too practical) and painting and nature and cleanliness and lovely things. Is adversely affected by such phenomena as pig pails etc.

g. Hopelessly bad at mathematics of any kind, tying knots and cutting bread.

h. Strong sense of and desire for adventure. In comparison with other people, certainly seems to attract it.

i. Very strong urge also (in relation to above) for travel. Dreams of Austria, Switzerland, Norway, Italy, Greece, Spain, South America, the West Indies, South Africa, Australia, New Zealand and the isles of the South Pacific. No hankerings at all for Canada, Yankeeland, India, Central Africa or most of North Africa, Malaya, Burma or Borneo.

j. Loves the open air and takes all possible. Adores sport in form of walking, riding, sailing (specially speed boats), cycling – pedal and otherwise – and is more than anxious to take up swimming. Indifferent to ball games and bad at them. Enjoys an afternoon's tennis but would rather lie in the shade if it's hot.

k. Needs a lot of sleep. Am at best on eight hours a night.

l. Much too critical. Also highly strung and sensitive.

m. No financial, social or career ambitions at all but is determined to live a full life and cram as much into it as humanly possible. Main fear: wasting time and youth.

n. Much too fastidious and critical to be a real flirt. Thus feelings go deep when attached. Definitely emotional.

o. Rather self-contained. Suffers sometimes from inner loneliness.

p. Reasonably considerate. Stupidly soft-hearted on occasions.

q. Rather too strongly developed sense of humour at times. Apt to lead to trouble. Was supposed to have been born laughing.

r. Fairly tidy but not methodically so.

s. Wants a reasonably sized family and will adore them.

t. No desire to live in large houses.

u. Very good with a needle.

v. Never gets boozy. Hates people who do and people who smoke too much and make you cough and blink and who are rude and who chew gum and who are loud and who swank.

w. Runs a mile from catty women and men who fancy themselves as lady killers (Notices that most officers do. Bad thing.)

x. Doesn't read an awful lot but a bit of a literary snob – incapable of enjoying trash.

y. Cries terribly in the cinema if film at all sad.

z. Has very high ideals on the subject of marriage and would throw the whole of herself into it to make it a success.

Well? Does my list tally? I'm not sure I'm wise telling you so much about myself!

12 January 1944   HMS *Shrapnel*, Southampton

We had fun this afternoon helping a diver to dress. You should see what he had to get into – poor man, I don't know how he moved at all. All sorts of screws had to be done up, things greased and goodness knows what before he was ready. Pam and I then turned the big wheel that sends down the oxygen. Something went wrong at one point and he floated to the top *horizontally*. I was petrified as I thought he was dead – but he wasn't.

20 January 1944   HMS *Shrapnel*, Southampton

My dearest

I'm feeling healthily and happily tired or, rather, sleepy. This morning I baled out two dinghies, did some rowing with Tim – duty officer had to be taken places – came back, made some cocoa, did a bit more rowing, went to the 'chippy' (carpenter) to get some toggles made, went to lunch, then spent the afternoon sitting on a large coil of rope sewing oars. Gosh, it was hard work. I was equipped with a leather 'palm', a needle four inches long, some double twine and the canvas. Heave, pull, tug . . . wield the beeswax to make the twine come through the canvas. Cor!

It was so beautiful on the water this morning, still and calm and misty with a pale pink light. I loved the exercise. I can row quite well with one oar but I cannot manage a boat singlehanded with two, nor can I scull with a flat oar in the stern. I'm just not that tough!

Rowing boats are not really our job. We're only on them because the speedboats aren't available. It makes a change.

I'm sure you're coming home this year but it's irksome waiting. When we first go out together in London we must go down and look at the river again. Do you remember our very first date, Eric? Meeting at Piccadilly by the Clock of the World, trying to find Jermyn Street and getting a bit lost, lovely dinner at *L'Ecu de France*, then coming out into the moonlight, walking down Lower Regent Street, down the Duke of York steps, through Admiralty Arch to Trafalgar Square, then down various ways to the Embankment. It was such a perfect night, wasn't it? Do you remember leaning on the parapet talking quietly and watching the little boats chug up and down. And then a ride in a tram as we both felt mad, then a taxi to the London Casino and dancing on the lovely stage and drinking Chablis and holding hands during the cabaret and then a walk down Oxford Street and a taxi ride to Bayswater. I'll never forget the atmosphere of it, ever.

Oh, dearest, just *think*, we might be together again soon!

23 January 1944   HMS *Shrapnel*, Southampton

My love, I nearly had kittens on Friday afternoon! We were out in the 48-foot long diesel, a rather cumbersome affair but fairly reliable. I was at the engine room controls when suddenly the naval officer aboard shouted out, 'Boggis, take over from Bolster. Bolster, take the wheel and be coxswain for half an hour.'

I've never had charge of a boat in my life. And not one that size into the bargain and a mixed crew to make it worse. I didn't know what to say. I climbed tremblingly up to the wheel, the other Wrens all agog with amusement, and off we went. I had to go alongside all sorts of things and do all sorts of manoeuvres, shouting instructions to the stoker – 'Half Ahead', 'Astern', 'Full Astern', 'Easy', 'Full Ahead'.

Then I had to answer the officer's questions – 'Yes, sir, wheel amidships.' 'Steamer on the starboard bow, sir, more than two points abaft the beam.'

I was *exhausted* by the time we got in. One day I'd love to be a coxswain but I want to prove myself an efficient stoker first.

1 February 1944 HMS *Tormentor*, Warsash, Hampshire

I have been drafted to another base on loan for a couple of weeks and yesterday I began my first twenty-four hour duty in boats' crews. Work? Dearest, we didn't stop. For eleven hours I stood over that engine heaving levers. I shall go to sleep tonight hearing coxswain's voice.

The boat was a cutter – Vosper V8 engine. I enjoyed it and the other girls were nice. It was lovely and romantic on the water last night – deep blue, black shapes, red and green lanterns, the lap lap of the water against boat sides and a cool breeze. It was pleasant to sit in a little hut between trips and make tea and toast on an anthracite stove.

14 February 1944 HMS *Tormentor*, Warsash, Hampshire

It's strange, you know, how life works out. While I've been on leave another girl has been stoking in my place. The other day she was standing where I'd have been standing in the boat when a great barrel of oil fell off the jetty, removing two of her fingers.

It might have been me . . .

15 February 1944 HMS *Tormentor*, Warsash, Hampshire

Dearest Eric

Tomorrow I go back with Maggie and Rozelle to Southampton. I've very mixed feelings about it – both places have their advantages but I must say this is a really lovely station.

I was on a smashing boat yesterday. We did nice trips, went gloriously fast and made lashings of coffee between runs. Last night we had a hectic evening drinking and dancing. This morning I go on duty again until 11.30 tonight.

I'll tell you what is stiff, though, and that's being bowman. You stand right up in the bows wielding an enormous heavy boat hook, throwing great wet ropes and catching them. One tiny slip, my love, and you're in the drink.

It's not much fun when you're hanging on for dear life with the hook to a boat you're alongside and coxswain suddenly moves forward and you can't get the hook away. Your arms are nearly torn out of their sockets.

Once yesterday I hadn't the sheer strength to hold on so I called out, 'Look out, I'm letting go the hook!' It swung alongside the other boat. A sailor kindly rescued it and passed it down to our sternman. But a beastly naval officer stood there with a sneer and said, 'I say, you really must look after those hooks, you know, they're expensive!'

I glared at him with what I hoped was contempt in my face.

20 February 1944   HMS *Shrapnel*, Southampton

Dearest

What a place this is, what goings on! What one could do if one wanted.

Our cabin, my love, is nearly opposite the phone room, so when the phone starts ringing one of us usually runs to answer it for the sake of peace. This is honestly typical of what happens every day.

This afternoon I answered it. A Yank voice said, 'Say, is Wren Goody there?' Whereupon I scoured the place for said Wren and, on being unsuccessful, returned to phone. This is the conversation that took place:

Me   'I'm so sorry but Wren Goody is out and won't be in till late.'
Yank 'Oh, that's too bad. Say, *you* doin' anything tonight?'
Me   'I'm afraid so.' (Visions of bed early)
Yank 'No kiddin'. Gotter date?'
Me   'Yes.' (Fingers crossed)
Yank 'Weeell, see, me and three other doughboys are mighty lonely and was wantin' some gals to go out with tonight. Would any of your friends come along?'

Me	(truthfully) 'All my friends are away on weekend leave or sleeping out passes.'
Yank	(getting a bit impatient) 'Say, can't you find us four reel nice dames from somewhere in your place? Would you mind askin'?'
Me	'Hold on please.' (Then enter recreation room and ask for any volunteers for a blind Yank date. There are no volunteers.)
Me	'So sorry, but the only Wrens in have made other arrangements and regret they can't come.'
Yank	'Aw, shucks, too bad. D'yer know where I can find some dames or where we can dance tonight?'
Me	'Well, being Sunday, it's impossible to find anywhere to dance, nor do I know where you could, er, find any girls . . .'
Yank	'Your voice is reel nice. I like it. What's your name?'
Me	'Gloria.' (Sudden inspiration on my part)
Yank	'Yeah, you sound like a Gloria. What's your other name?'
Me	'Gorgeous.'
Yank	'Gloria Gorgeous! Oh my! See yah. G'dbye.'

This evening I came off duty and went to the regulating office. I was waiting my turn to speak to the petty officer when I overheard talk of a huge Yank soldier who had been in demanding to see a Wren called Gloria Gorgeous. He refused to believe there wasn't one, became abusive and had to be removed.

I kept very quiet.

22 February 1944   HMS *Shrapnel*, Southampton

Dearest Eric

It seems I'll have to do some explaining on the noble profession of stoking! You see, in the old days the stoker was the chap who shovelled all the coal down below in the big ships. Then, with the advent of the great diesels and turbines, there was less of that to do and the stoker became an engine room mechanic. Today the stoker knows all about engines, repairs, maintenance etc and he's quite a skilled man, especially when he gets to chief stoker, which is about the most highly paid non-commissioned job in the service.

My job, dearest, is being entirely responsible for the engine on whatever boat I happen to be. I must start it, stop it and drive it, fill up with fuel and lubricating oil, clean and mend it. For instance,

I've spent today on a snappy craft with an 8-cylinder Vosper engine. When I went aboard this morning I saw to the petrol, oil and water-cooling system. I cleaned the weed trap, pumped the bilge, rubbed up the brasses with polish, tightened a couple of screws, greased a nut, then ran her for a bit until she sailed.

I stood at the controls while coxswain steered with the tiller and Pam and Tim wielded boat hooks and threw ropes and made fast. Have you got it clear, dearest? I think it's the best job going. People at home make all sorts of comments, for example, 'My dear, how *comic*,' 'I suppose you shovel coal all day,' 'Funny you haven't ruined your hands,' 'How quaint, fancy you being a stoker, ha, ha,' 'What a far cry from dress designing . . .'

I don't get dirty, at least not specially. My trousers aren't nearly as grubby as the deckhands', who are always handling wet ropes. I've kept my hands all right, too, though it's meant taking great care of them.

At Warsash we had a lot of practice in boat handling – pulling the boat alongside with boat hooks, rope throwing, catching and tying and, horror of horrors, mooring the craft that came in. That meant jumping off the boat onto awful buoys bobbing about in the water and doing frantically difficult things with great heavy wires. I can't tell you what it was like at night when you had to do it in the pitch black with only one hand because you had to hold an Aldis lamp in the other. I just don't know how I never fell in. (It's quite a common occurrence.) I did like the deckhand work as it was fun to perch in the bows while sailing – but I was glad to get back to an engine.

Talking of doing deckhand at Warsash, we went out one day to a boat which had some Yank sailors aboard and one of them caught my line for me and made fast. He was inclined to be chatty so, for something to say, I asked him what his boat was like. He paused for a moment or two, chewing gum and looking me up and down, then drawled, 'Say, what do you mean what's my *bed* like?' I was *livid*. Everyone looked round and stared. A beastly sub-lieutenant was splitting his sides and there was me trying so pathetically hard to be dignified in my bell bottoms with the wind blowing my hair in all directions!

Dearest Eric

Please come and cheer me up. I've just left Sick Bay after a flu-cold and I could die with depression. I know it's silly.

We're none of us well. Southampton is about the most unhealthy place imaginable – low-lying, damp and foggy. At Portsmouth and Warsash to catch cold was unheard of and 'not done' in boats' crews. In fact at *Hornet*, a famous naval base, the Wren crews there did not have one case to report at Sick Bay the whole winter.

Here, though, it's not so good. We're not well fed, the base is damp and so our boating clothes are damp when we put them on. We work in warm clothes all day, then in the cold of the evening we must take them off to come home as the first officer doesn't like to see Wrens in bell bottoms. We feel fine while actually out on the water. Then we come back to this great hotel, to a fug so thick we can hardly breathe, no matter how wide we open the windows.

Poor old Roz has a sore throat, Pam a streaming cold and Tim a hacking cough, so I've got company in my depression.

Dearest, do you ever long for after the war? For civilian life, for civilian clothes, for home life and lovely things around you and rooms with flowers in them and privacy and – and freedom – to go where you like when you like and have quietness when you want it.

I shall look back on my sailing days with a slight pang, I'm sure, and something inside me will always yearn for the sea and the gulls' cries and the rise and fall of a boat when you are up forward in the bows and the sense of excitement as you open up with the throttle and feel the craft leap ahead beneath you and the old tars who tell you their tales and the things you do with knots and flags and the sight of big ships.

It will always have glamour for me as long as I live.

I don't think I told you about Rozelle's and my 'happy' afternoon this week – I don't believe I did. Well, we had orders to take some stores out to a vessel down the water. We set forth in the open cutter with our leading seaman coxswain, me working the engine and Roz in the bows. We came alongside and made secure. They got the stuff off, then returned to find some other stores for us to take back.

I expect you know, dearest, that when a large boat goes along it leaves a wash in its wake and it's up to a small boat to avoid getting in the middle of it.

Suddenly one of the sailors cried, 'For Gawd's sake, look out!' I looked behind me and there was a great tug affair coming up on our stern, passing far too close, with the hell of a wash behind it.

Before you could blink we were in the middle of it – thrown up into the air and down again like a cork, bashed against the side of the other vessel till every board creaked and groaned. The fire extinguisher went for six, everything was rolling about in the bottom and Roz was hanging on for dear life in the bows as white as a sheet.

Coxswain was vainly trying to ward off the blows as we crashed against the other boat. I struggled to turn off ignition knobs and petrol cocks and keep jars of oil upright and myself in the boat. More and more enormous waves kept coming – we thought they'd never stop before the cutter was broken in two. There was an awful lot of shouting and swearing. At last peace reigned and we surveyed the damage – the starboard side hopelessly bashed, the bows badly dented.

We were just recuperating from this when out of a hole in the side of the vessel we were alongside poured a cascade of sewage, water and muck – whoosh – all over our boat and narrowly missing me. I called out for a rating to come and clean it up, please. Quite a nice lad climbed down with a bucket, then of course he had to go and drop it in the ocean. Awful panic trying to rescue it with a boat hook, during which Coxswain fell in. It was really incredible.

A little while later Roz and I were quietly chatting in the stern sheets when a sub-lieutenant RNVR aged about thirty-five to forty came aboard. He looked us up and down and got talking. Oh, we worked round 'ere did we? Fancy that. 'Ow would I like to 'ave lunch aboard his ship tomorrow? Like to entertain me, 'e would.

I said I didn't know what my duties were to be so couldn't make arrangements. 'Oh – well 'ow about a nice evenin' out dancin' tonight?' I said I had a filthy cold and was turning in early (quite true). He got annoyed then and told me I didn't seem to know my own mind. I said quietly that I resented personal remarks and he threw a lump of coal at my cheek!

2 March 1944   H M S *Shrapnel*, Southampton

We caught fire yesterday. Flames suddenly leapt from the petrol pump on the starboard engine and, almost simultaneously, the port engine started a fire as well. We've had the boat officer aboard and he got so hicked up it was a treat. The deckhands were perched up on the cabin roof laughing like drains and Maggie and I were doing things with fire extinguishers and handfuls of cotton waste. She got a bit burnt but I didn't.

Then one of the petty officers was coxswaining and he went and jammed the gears. You never heard anything like the bangs and explosions going on in the engine room.

I thought we'd all be blown up.

10 March 1944   H M S *Shrapnel*, Southampton

Dearest Eric

Am a bit under the weather if the truth be told. Had a rather hectic evening out last night, ending in thirty minutes' steady sprinting through the streets of Southampton to get in in time with all the Yanks and *hoi polloi* yelling at us. I don't think I've ever run so hard in all my life. Rozelle kept saying from behind in awful gasps, 'Maureen, *do* stop . . . I shall drop dead . . . I . . . shall . . . drop . . . dead . . .'

We landed in a heap by the sentry just as the clock was striking. It was a bit much to have to crawl up 130 steps on top of all that!

I think my days in Southampton are coming to an end. Warsash have asked to have me back permanently and I think I'm going. I'm quite glad. This is an awfully low-lying spot, very damp and unhealthy – and miserably squalid in parts. Warsash lies between Southampton and Portsmouth at the bottom of Southampton Water and is very beautiful.

Rozelle is coming too, I understand, but the worst of it is Maggie will be left behind, so our lovely threesome will be broken up.

I've been very happy here and have had good companionship and fun. One good thing, dearest, Warsash does give compassionate leave easily and their Wren CO is understanding. There've been five deserters here since Christmas, all married girls going off to be with their husbands because they weren't allowed leave.

We moved our cabin this morning and now have a lovely view

over the docks and the water. I wish it was nearer the real sea but the cries of the gulls make you think you are actually on the coast.

My goodness, Eric, we *have* got a pest of a boat officer. He's a sub-lieutenant RNVR, about thirty, married with one child. He's fair with protruding round eyes and loose lips. He really is the end. We literally have to avoid going near him – he takes every opportunity to slip an arm around one and several times has tried to kiss Pam and me. I can't tell you how revolting he is.

Pam had an awful time with him the other day, edging round and round the wheelhouse in *Anndora* to get away from him. He's taken to calling me 'dear' when alone and he even pinched Tim's situpon. We all *loathe* him – and being so wrapped up in his own conceit he just can't see it. You really should see his leer. It's too good to be true. He swears like a dockyard thug and has a really bad temper – also is too fond of the whisky bottle. We treated him as a sort of joke at first but it's going a bit far now.

Wot one puts up with for the sake of patriotism!

Cheerio,

love

O Love X
O love X
O love X
O Love X
O Love X
O Lov. X

Maureen

P.S. I Love You

P.S:- I love you!

143

13 March 1944   HMS *Shrapnel*, Southampton

Dearest Eric

Your letter of 29 February to hand. It's been much censored, place names eradicated, but I gather you're somewhere around Algiers. You know, I hope you realise how lucky you are to see all these exciting places, dearest. Come and look out of the window with me a moment. It's the Wrens' mess window of the base where we work. Just below there's a filthy mud swamp with a few old derelict rowing boats lying half bogged. To the left is the water, to the right a row of squalid dockers' cottages. As far as the eye can see there's bomb damage. Over there a factory chimney is belching black smoke.

Having carefully examined your letter again I've been able to decipher the word 'Algiers'. Goodness, I do hope you'll get back from there. Be careful, dearest, and don't go down any side streets, please, as I hear there's a lot of knifing going on. We've been told all sorts of yarns by sailors about the place. Apparently the people are very dirty and smelly, especially the French. Do you really think they will send you home from there for a time?

I'm still expecting to go back to Warsash this week, though whether temporarily or permanently I don't know. In a way Southampton's all right. There are one or two nice hotels and plenty of cinemas but Warsash has other attractions. I feel sort of fifty-fifty about it really – I'm quite ready to take what fate will give me.

Later. I've had it, chum – off to Warsash tomorrow with Roz and Tim. Visions of frantic packing rush before my eyes.

Have spent today in sou'wester and oilskins baling the bilges in the pouring rain. You were *damn* lucky to go in with a commission, my love. You don't know what we rankers put up with!

Still, I wouldn't be a Wren officer for anything in the world.

17 March 1944   HMS *Tormentor*, Warsash, Hampshire

Dearest Eric

Here I am, back again where I was before. I'm so happy about it. It's beautiful here, I'd love to show it to you. I've done my first duty watch – from midday yesterday till midday today. I've been so content. I love the place, the boats, the scenery, the other girls, the quarters.

I'm in a clean little private house taken over. I look out of the window of my cabin on a really lovely view. And, dearest, who do you think I'm in a cabin with? Lord Louis Mountbatten's daughter, Patricia, her friend, Anne Curzon-Howe (father an admiral too)[1] and two other girls, Pamela Ward, who is very tall and in gunnery, and Molly O'Kelly, who comes from Kildare.

They're all so nice, I can't get over it. I dote on them. They put bottles in my bed when I come off late duty and are so considerate and friendly. It's quite a crazy cabin and there's much laughing and eating. An amazing collection of records are continually being played on Patricia's ancient gramophone. She has Tino Rossi singing 'J'attendrai', 'My Bill', 'The Lady is a Tramp', 'Boum' (our first dance together, remember?) but best of all I love her record of the Tchaikovsky 'Serenade for Strings'. It is hauntingly beautiful.

Tonight it's been 'J'attendrai' and it made me long for you. It's spring, dearest, glorious surging spring. I felt quite drunk on the boats this morning with sun and wind and spray and blue sky and the smell of the sea.

Rozelle and Tim are here too. Roz and I went back to Southampton this morning to collect some things and it seemed so constricted and cramped after these wide open spaces.

Every other night I have to work till nearly midnight. Think of me driving my engine beneath the stars, getting sleepier and sleepier, then tottering up to the quarters and climbing into bed in the dark. I prefer to have my evenings free but it can't be helped. I'm on a cutter at the moment with a coxswain and a deckhand.

Eric, if you send me a cable send it to WREN BOLSTER, HMS 'TORMENTOR', C/O GPO. It's an exciting address, isn't it?

19 March 1944 HMS *Tormentor*, Warsash, Hampshire

It's a grand place this! I'm revelling in it. We positively live on the boats and I only wish I could tell you all about everything but the censorship's terribly strict.

It's funny, you know, when you're used to running about on boats and being out of doors you tend to forget that other people are a bit nervous aboard and feel the cold. Yesterday afternoon it

[1] In fact a captain – Leicester Charles Assheton St John Curzon-Howe, 1894–1941. Naval Attaché, British Embassy, Washington, 1938–1941.

was warm and sunny with a fair breeze. We were all in trousers and plimsolls and jerseys (no coats) and lying alongside the jetty for a few minutes. Suddenly along came a party of airmen and Waafs armed with hockey sticks. Something had gone wrong with their transport so we had to ferry them. We were nearly splitting our sides – each one had to be helped in, they were falling all over the place and sitting down plop. They were wearing greatcoats with their collars turned up to their ears. They stood there muffled up and absolutely goggling at us. We had to help them off at the other end. I suppose I was like that once . . .

I don't know, Eric, when it's loveliest out on the water – in the early morning when it's all misty and still and pearly or midday with the sun shining and glistening on everything and it almost hurts your eyes to look over the stern at the wash. I think perhaps it's best at twilight when the sun is setting and the stars come one by one and the lights go on and night falls gradually. It's exciting later on too when it's really dark and you're more conscious of the noise of the water lapping against the sides of the boat and you can't see much but the lights and dark shapes moving silently and you can count the stars as you go along.

I love being a stoker. On the cutter I'm on at present the 'engine room' is on deck, in the stern. When it's fine we let the canvas walls and ceiling down. I enjoy having the engine in my control, opening up and feeling the boat leap ahead.

I had a terrific clean up yesterday afternoon and I swear there's not a cleaner engine than mine on the whole south coast!

21 March 1944   HMS *Tormentor*, Warsash, Hampshire

Dearest

Two airgraphs and the copy of your second application for home posting. That really should have melted their hearts. Oh why didn't it? Perhaps it will yet. Shall I write? I'm sure that would help.

Sir – Please send my chap home because I love him and I haven't seen him for over three years and I'm sure he'd be much more use in England and if *you* loved anyone like I love him you'd agitate like mad to have him home and he really has had his fair share of life in the East and I promise we'll both be awfully good if you send my chap home.

Signed hopefully
Eric's girlfriend

Tear round dotted line and dispatch by post.

Well, dearest, I guess there's nothing for me to do but go on hoping and waiting and you to go on trying and being nice to them wot deals in these matters. I really have a deep faith that we will be together, though this waste of time and youth riles me immeasurably.

I'm sunburnt already and in exuberant health – quite 'bonny boats' crew', to use a loathsome expression.

Last night, in the dark, I had to do bowman for a change. Perilous business of jumping onto strange jetties with ropes without being able to see where you're jumping to. I'd rather attend to my engine than do antics in the black-out but sometimes it can't be helped.

I had my first nightmare last night – at least what I mean is the first for a very long time. I awoke the whole cabin by yelling 'Anne! Anne!' at the top of my voice. I'd sat up in the middle of a horrid dream, caught my hair on the springs of the bunk above me and thought I'd got entangled in the rope netting that hangs off the sides of ships. I was therefore yelling for my coxswain to help me. I was half out of bed by this time when Patricia Mountbatten's sleepy voice broke in on my semi-consciousness, 'It's all right, dear, go sleep. You're at *Tormentor.*'

Such an apt remark under the circumstances. Pam Ward started to giggle and apparently I said, 'Oh Lor, I'm having a nightmare, so sorry,' and subsided. This is a lovely quiet cabin – no snorers, tooth-grinders, coughers or talkers.

I had an off-morning today. I kept tripping up and dropping things just when the bosun was looking – and I got a bottle for leaving a scrubbing brush in a pail of water.

3 April 1944   Sick Bay, HMS *Tormentor*, Warsash, Hampshire

Dearest

You will have noticed a gap in my letters. I'm afraid I haven't been able to write for some time because I've been having typhoid!

Eleven days ago I was inoculated. I went straight on duty afterwards and was took very queer. I was brought to Sick Bay in an ambulance. It's the oddest thing, because my first inoculation a year ago didn't affect me at all and I was the only one this time who gave out.

Apparently they inoculate you with the disease and something's supposed to counteract it. In my case for some unknown reason nothing did the counteracting, so I got left holding the baby, or rather the typhoid. I'm fed up with it – I've had fever and temperatures and sore throat and horrible sickness and gyppy tum. However, they treated me with belladonna and it's done me a lot of good. I'm on an egg and milk diet now. I'm furious because I've felt marvellous since I got here.

Rozelle comes every day to see me, Patricia Mountbatten brings me eggs and apples and chocolate – so does Anne Curzon-Howe. Nearly all the boats' crews have been up. I've really been awfully spoilt by my chums.

15 April 1944   HMS *Tormentor*, Warsash, Hampshire

I can't *think* what will happen to us if you get back very soon. There's a sickening story in circulation about a Wren whose fiancé is in London. They can't meet as he can't get into the banned area and she can't leave it! (You'll have seen in the papers about this wonderful coastal ban.)

A Wren here is getting married tomorrow. Fortunately her husband's here too. But her mother cannot come down to see her child married as it's in the coastal area. The police won't let her.

It's the same all over the country.

20 April 1944   HMS *Tormentor*, Warsash, Hampshire

Last night, about 9.30, I wandered into a base dance. Everyone is agreed that it went off marvellously. No one was left sitting out at all. It was hot in there, dreadfully hot. And crowded. Through the haze of cigarette smoke one could see the imported band producing its cacophony. One was pushed and shoved amid other pushing and shoving people – people with red perspiring faces, people with beery breath, people with sleeves rolled up, everyone getting down to the business of enjoying themselves.

In the corners couples were jitterbugging, the men with glazed expressions, the Wrens with funny smirks. There was a distinct smell of bodies. A few officers with supercilious and self-satisfied expressions pushed and shoved with the rest. By a quarter to eleven my ankles were bruised and aching and my eyes sore from the atmosphere, so I came away.

The feel of the rain on my face was wonderful as I stepped into the night.

23 April 1944   HMS *Tormentor*, Warsash, Hampshire

I must tell you something that happened this afternoon. You know I told you the officers here are a twerpish crowd. Well, I was on duty in the boats' crew hut and talking to a rather unpleasantish workmate when in came a twerp sub-lieutenant full of his own conceit and behaving as if he owned the Royal Navy.

I saw through him at a glance. Never having seen me before, he began to get familiar but got nowhere. The other girl was throwing her sex at him so he tried to date up with her (bad form in front of me). He went on being absolutely frightful. The other girl said, 'Do you know any of the Wren boats' crews at X?' 'Oh God, yes,' he said, 'had dates with all of them but couldn't keep them, had too many on shore.'

I don't know what possessed me but I said, rather sarcastically, 'You must be a perfect Don Juan!' Twerp simply horrified. Exit twerp slowly out of door in silence.

26 April 1944   HMS *Tormentor*, Warsash, Hampshire

I'm sitting on the floor in front of a primus stove and Patricia Mountbatten's little wireless exudes Verdi – glorious, emotional, breathtaking Verdi. It's no wonder I feel more in love with you than ever at the moment!

This is a very beautiful place. I've never seen such masses of magnificent flowering shrubs.

This afternoon I knew wild exhilaration as I had a long-distance trip in a powerful speedboat – blue sky, blue water, foam, wind, speed. Just Cynthia Gudgeon as coxswain and me. I had to be more than a little nippy coping with bows and stern as well.

It was marvellous! Unfortunately coming in on our return there was a tricky bit of manoeuvring to do and our boss (fearsome man) started yelling and screaming at us. Cynthia, of course, began to giggle and, what with trying not to and getting somewhat flustered, I was a bit slow with a spot of rope throwing. At the top of his voice, in front of hordes of folk, he shouted and roared, 'Aargh! Aargh! You two are as helpless as two bloody cats trying to swim the Atlantic!'

Sweet thing . . .

1 May 1944   HMS *Tormentor*, Warsash, Hampshire

My dearest
The first of May – the first of May already. It can't be long now. I find it hard to take it in that England, my country, is on the verge of her greatest campaign of all time. It's too immense, too shattering.

I hardly dare think what it will mean, the lives that will be lost, the numbers of everything involved – ships, planes, armour, men. One waits impatiently, wanting to get the strain of waiting over yet dreading it.

The weather has been so wonderful, it's made it all the harder to understand the way of things. Every time I see a soldier I look at him, remembering what he has ahead of him and it shakes me.

Everyone is expectant, unsettled. Some sailors I spoke to yesterday had the usual philosophy of the sea. 'Yeah, wish it'd hurry up and come off, then we'll get our leave quicker!'

It must be desperately exciting for all the people in the occupied countries who are genuinely anti-German.

I've sprained my foot and am hobbling around pathetically with it all bound up. It's a common thing among boats' crewites – the result of all the leaping about in plimsolls. It's the easiest thing in the world to jump on a bit of rope or a slippery patch or land on the wrong foot or something. It'll only last a few days.

Oh, the warrant officer bosun is a horrid man, Eric. I hate him because he shouts so and scares me. He says such revolting things to one. I simply hadn't the force in my arm to throw a great hefty rope an awful distance yesterday – the bowline, actually – and I kept throwing just short of the mark. That brute bent over the rail and bellowed scathingly, 'I must say, your parents must be *very* proud of you!'

He then informed me that I had the intelligence of a louse.

21 May 1944 HMS *Tormentor*, Warsash, Hampshire

Of course the Wrens in Algiers haven't heard of Wren stokers – we're frightfully select. There aren't more than forty of us in the whole service. If you tell people I'm in boats' crews they'll understand better. We're the most snooty category – about the hardest to get in to – and we have to contend with a lot of jealousy, especially from the office crowd.

My friend Cynthia was coxswaining a cutter the other day when something, I can't gather quite what, went wrong with the fuel and water systems. The boat began to sink and the poor girl was overcome by the fumes. I believe she and her crew of one or two were rescued just in time.

Glad I wasn't involved in that.

5 June 1944   HMS *Tormentor*, Warsash, Hampshire

We are gated. No one can phone in or out. Dearest Eric, I probably won't even try and send this letter to you for several days.

Our craft have all slipped away.

Still, we are not absolutely sure it's the real thing as the weather is so cold, grey and windy. Some are wondering if it is another big exercise like the recent 'Fabius',[1] but in my heart I'm sure.

I'm trying not to think of individuals – the crew of 516, the stripey[2] off 515, that sparks with the lovely smile, Pixie McNab's boyfriend, the big bearded Jock . . . so many marvellous young men.

I am haunted by the memory of passing the soccer field the other day and seeing masses of commando lads resting with tin helmets and kit. Some were lying asleep in the sun. They looked so young I could hardly bear it and tears ran down my cheeks. Where are they now?

Patricia has gone on night duty.

Anne is silent.

Pam, Moll and I are restless and I doubt if we'll sleep well tonight.

7 June 1944   HMS *Tormentor*, Warsash, Hampshire

My dearest

Well, we've had our D-Day, so long awaited and worked and striven for.

I wish I could give you an impression of what the atmosphere has been here – and still is. It's something I wouldn't have missed for anything on earth.

I expect this high excitement and tremendous tension will give way to bad temper and flatness when reaction sets in. It was impossible to work yesterday. We stood about chatting, wondering, hungry for any scraps of news, hovering between wireless and windows.

Last night Patricia Mountbatten and I went for a walk on the shore and from the south-west came the distant rumblings of guns.

Some poor things are frantic with worry over fiancés, boyfriends

---

[1] The codename for a major dress rehearsal of the D-Day landings which was carried out on the south coast early in May.

[2] A rating with the maximum of three good conduct badges (stripes).

and brothers. Nearly everyone feels anxiety about the menfolk we all know from here.

Planes have roared and roared overhead – great heavy bombers streaming south and the less noisy fighters.

Few people slept well the night before or last night. It's all been such a tremendous thing.

I can't tell you what it was like to land back here on the eve of the Second Front – from home, where the war is something utterly remote and village life goes on undisturbed in its tranquillity. It was a shattering experience.

It gives me an elated feeling, dearest, as if we've turned the most vital corner of the war and there, ahead, lies peace beyond the immediate battles – and everything that it *must* mean for you and me.

Did you by any chance hear the King's speech and nine o'clock news from London last night? It was the most stirring and perfectly done hour of broadcasting I've ever heard. It moved me to the core.

One girl here doesn't know if she's coming or going as she's heard that we've dropped parachutists on the Channel Isles,[1] where her home and all her people are. She alone got away – four years ago.

I wish, Eric, I could tell you the story of what we know and have seen but, of course, I can't. When it's all past history I'll describe it to you dramatically over Chablis when we're dining out.

9 June 1944   HMS *Tormentor*, Warsash, Hampshire

Dearest Eric

My goodness, I wouldn't be on leave at this time! Thank God everything is going quite well.

It's wonderful to see the men coming back, dirty, unshaven, some suffering from shock in varied degrees, others cheerful and wanting to get back. They all have tremendous tales to tell.

One officer got back here from a port on another coast wearing his officer's cap, flannel bags, a dreadful old jacket and moth-eaten brown carpet slippers! Another broadcast last night on the nine o'clock news. Perhaps you heard him.

---

[1] This rumour was incorrect. The Allied invasion forces by-passed the Channel Islands and they were not liberated until the very end of the war in Europe.

We've been on the films too. The first invasion newsreel! Naturally the place is a hotbed of rumours and I only wish I could tell you what we know to be true.

On Wednesday night there was a dance here. Heaven knows I didn't feel like dancing with all that hell going on not so very far away, but something inside told me to go and help bring a little gaiety to relieve the tenseness of the atmosphere. So another Wren and I went along.

I'm glad I went. I hadn't been there long when a young lad slipped into the hall and sat beside me. I took one look and I knew where he'd been. His eyes were bloodshot and red-rimmed and he was shaking like a leaf. He was just an ordinary seaman.

Poor kid, all he could say was, 'Make me forget it, please make me forget it. I've just got to.' I felt quite sick with pity, Eric. I looked after him all evening. He'd just had his nineteenth birthday. At first he was incoherent but as I yattered trivialities he gradually got better. He was upset because his mother would be worried. What that kid had seen was beyond telling. For one thing he had seen his special pals blown to pieces.

By the end of the evening he could hardly stand for exhaustion, so I put him in the care of a petty officer, who promised to put him to bed. Just as I was leaving three ruffians came in. Filthy, bleary-eyed and unshaven, they just stood there. No one seemed to take any notice of them. I didn't know them but I went up and said, 'Hullo, I'm *terribly* glad to see you back.' One just looked at me and sort of sobbed, 'God, you don't know how pleased we are to see *you* stokie!' Nothing one can do for these men is too much.

Lots of German prisoners have been turning up in these parts. Rozelle has seen hundreds of them. She said they look awful – just like animals.

We thought we'd be bombed all along the coast but nothing's happened.

12 June 1944   HMS *Tormentor*, Warsash, Hampshire

I had a good day yesterday. I went over to the port where I was before I came here and had an uproarious time with Roz and Maggie. I must say our threesome is the best thing I've got out of the service. I love those two and we all understand each other perfectly. We like the same people and, what is more, we dislike the same people! Moreover we have the same taste in entertainment and are all stokers.

We went to the part of the docks where Roz now operates from and I got a trip in a fast boat with her. We went careering along with me stoking in a skirt and silk stockings.

It was *quite* riveting in that dockyard. I could sit there all day and watch. I doubt whether there's any spot in England quite so interesting at this time.

My goodness, I've been lucky to be on this stretch of the coast of all parts of England. We've really felt a part of operations here. It's been a perfect miracle of organisation, Eric. Civilians living ten miles inland hardly know there's a war on. Mails have continued as normal and passenger trains have been little changed.

Occasionally one comes across a line of tanks parked by the roadside. It's fun to read what's chalked up on them. 'Heaven Can Wait (I Hope)', 'Book me that bedroom suite', 'French women, wine and song!' 'Comment allez vous – vous êtes jolie . . .'

We passed some in a street yesterday. A little urchin girl clasping a coat around her ran up to one of the tank drivers and said, 'Say, mister, guess wot colour dress I got on.' The man said, 'Oh, blue?' Whereupon the child threw open her coat to disclose a skinny and naked little torso, said, 'Yah, got yer,' and ran away.

It was some business walking through the dockyard. The small number of Wrens there are the only women to be seen. Oh dear . . . 'Ere, Curly, I'll give yer two pounds for ternight.' 'Like ter come in my tank, dear?' 'Nah then, don't blush!' 'Look, mates, stoker first class and nice legs too.' 'That's right, dear, try not ter laugh.' They're all so brave and cheerful those men. All one could do was to give them a wave and a grin.

I've got a nasty suspicion that one may soon have a sad feeling of anti-climax and flatness, all that we've striven for and waited for having happened. One wonders what will become of us. It will never be the same here again.

Meanwhile there's much of interest going on. Our sick bay has had Jerry officers and French women snipers (for our side). Boats' crews girls have worked hard bringing in wounded. Daily one hears good and bad news of craft one knows of. All this means the war may soon be over . . .

13 June 1944 HMS *Tormentor*, Warsash, Hampshire

My coxswain, dearest, is a treat. We call her 'Pongo' because she was four years in the ATS. She's thirty-three and as tough as an old boot. She has short cropped hair, weather-beaten face, nobbly hands and a hearty manner. She has one love in life and that is boats. It's all she lives for.

She's a good sort really – trying at times – and gets a hell of a lot of work out of us but, my God, she's funny. She climbs into the cutter in the morning and says, 'Good morning, *Sea Mouse*. How are you, dear? Come along, *Sea Mousey*, we're going for a little trip. That's right . . . round . . . round . . . Yes, *Sea Mouse*, I believe you'll behave today.'

She rolls her trousers up and runs about barefoot and yells vile abuse at any form of boat that so much as grazes the side of her *Sea Mouse*.

She's the perfect example of a real tough sporting Englishwoman such as the French cartoonists adore.

17 June 1944 HMS *Tormentor*, Warsash, Hampshire

Dearest Eric

I got your letters of 6 and 7 June when I came off watch. *Please*, Eric, don't let this fall through. I couldn't bear it if it did. Please do everything you can so that they don't forget or go and find you another job or something. Just come, anyway, by the first plane leaving for England.

I've warned Mummy to expect you any time.

I've been to the first officer and explained the situation. She was as nice as could be and said she'd do her best to get me compassionate leave. She will, I know – she's very human about these things.

Dearest, if by some chance it should fall through don't ever tell me again that you're coming unless it's absolutely a hundred per cent sure and you're all packed and waiting for the plane.

I couldn't bear another crisis.

Oh Eric, dearest Eric, do you really think you'll be home soon?

I hope you won't get this letter.

I hope you'll have left before it arrives.

All the time I keep sending up little prayers, 'Please let him come home safely!'

All the time I was baling out filthy, stinking bilges today I was dreaming such beautiful dreams.

Then, when I was wending my way up the long path to Hook Bye, going off duty, I heard it.

Buzz bomb. You know what happens? As long as you hear that horrid buzz buzz . . . buzz, buzz, you know it's going over and some other unfortunate is going to cop it.

I couldn't see it because of low grey cloud.

It cut out.

I flung myself down and rolled under a bush and lay face down, trying to protect my head. It flashed through my mind how stupid it would be for me to be killed just as it looks as if you really will be home soon.

The explosion was shattering. We don't know much yet. It is thought that no one from the base has been killed, but we believe the surgeon's house was lost.

I'm writing this feeling very dazed and overwhelmed and wishing with all my strength and waiting very hopefully.

I so long to hear your voice.

POSTSCRIPT

At the end of June 1944 Squadron Leader Eric Wells returned to England on a posting to the Air Ministry.

On 8 July he and Maureen were married. Cabinmates Molly, Pam and Patricia attended the wedding. Stokers Anne, Margaret and Rozelle were unable to get leave.

After the war Eric and Maureen went to Australia and settled in Melbourne. They had a son and three daughters.

Maureen is still entertaining Eric.

Photographs

Eric's favourite photograph of Maureen, taken in December 1940

Eric Wells, 1942

Surgeon Commander (later Surgeon Captain) F Bolster CMG MD RN

*The author (right) with her mother, Mrs Violet Bolster,
and Joy the fox terrier at Compton, 1942*

Weydown House, Haslemere (HMS Mercury I*), 1943*

Margaret Boggis

Rozelle Pierrepont

WRNS boats' crew

The author (left) with Rozelle Pierrepont and Margaret Boggis

Bosun's crew, HMS Tormentor, *1944*
Back row, extreme left, Pamela de Castro ('Pongo'); fourth from left, the author.
Front row, second from left, Cynthia Gudgeon

Patricia Mountbatten

Anndora II (on left) at Southampton

Mary Benwell ('Benny') and Pamela Desoutter

Pamela Desoutter and Tim Edridge

A boats' crew Wren leaps ashore

Boats' crew Wren with boat hook

*Landing craft carrying men of the
1st Special Service (Commando) Brigade setting out from Warsash
for the Normandy beaches on D-Day, 6 June 1944*

Wedding reception, Compton,
8 July 1944.
Left to right: Pamela Ward,
Patricia Mountbatten, Molly
O'Kelly, Maureen and Eric Wells,
Charles Raynor

Eric and Maureen on honeymoon,
July 1944

COURIER POEM

This poem really wrote itself. On a warm June day in 1943 I was
somewhere between Crewe and Stafford in a very old train which
rattled mercilessly. As I sat gazing out of the window in
contemplative mood the rhythm of the wheels – dig a dig dig …
dig a dig dig – took form:

Here I am, here I am, here I am again,
What could be nicer than sitting in a train?
Rattling on to Birmingham, Manchester or Crewe,
It's all so exciting I don't know what to do!
Shall I go to Liverpool, Hull or Plymouth Hoe?
It's even further still to go right up to Scapa Flow.
And Ponders End's 'experience' and Glossop may lack charm,
But a job to Milford Haven would not do me any harm.
Perhaps I'll go to Greenock and go aboard a ship,
Though dispatches to the Admiralty's a most exciting trip.
If I go across to Derry I may very well be sick,
The Isle of Man is just as bad, it's not the job I'd pick.
Nothing can compare, of course, with the COLOSSAL fun
Of sitting in a train all night digesting tea and bun,
Or arriving where I have to go at 0 four 00 hours,
Then bleary eyed and grubby faced exerting all my powers
To charm the factory manager or PRDFO.
While wondering how quickly he is going to let me go.
And naturally it's much more fun to have in my fond charge
Enormous quantities of gear, both small and very large.
Twenty something hundredweight means nothing to me now,
I'm the darling of the porters from Aberdeen to Slough.
Travelling first is very nice and makes me feel quite grand,
And I've met some funny people as I'm sure you'll understand.
I find the army stolid, while the RAF is not,
And the Royal Navy is quite definitely HOT!
I'm a great success with business men, and gold braid I adore,
But the glamour does wear rather thin when they begin to snore.

175

Now why not be a courier? I leave you with this thought,
I can guarantee excitement, though never mind what sort!
So pack your bag and follow me and very soon you'll be,
If not a perfect Bradshaw, then a walking A B C.

788